Groups as Agents

Key Concepts in Philosophy Series

Groups as Agents

Deborah Perron Tollefsen

polity

The right of Deborah Perron Tollefsen to be identified as Author of this Work has been asserted in accordance with the UK Copyright, Designs and Patents Act 1988.

First published in 2015 by Polity Press

Polity Press
65 Bridge Street
Cambridge CB2 1UR, UK

Polity Press
350 Main Street
Malden, MA 02148, USA

ISBN-13: 978-0-7456-8483-3
ISBN-13: 978-0-7456-8484-0 (pb)

A catalogue record for this book is available from the British Library.

Library of Congress Cataloging-in-Publication Data

Tollefsen, Deborah.
   Groups as agents / Deborah Perron Tollefsen.
      pages cm
   Includes bibliographical references and index.
   ISBN 978-0-7456-8483-3 (hardback : alk. paper) – ISBN 978-0-7456-8484-0 (pbk. : alk. paper)   1. Act (Philosophy)   2. Agent (Philosophy)   3. Social groups.   I. Title.
   B105.A35T65 2015
   128'.4–dc23
                                        2014036747

Typeset in 10.5 on 12 pt Sabon
by Toppan Best-set Premedia Limited
Printed and bound in the by CPI Group (UK) Ltd, Croydon, CRO 4YY

Contents

Preface and Acknowledgments

In the social sciences and in everyday speech we often talk about groups as if they behaved in the same way as individuals, thinking and acting as a singular being. We say, for example, that "Google intends to develop an automated car," "the US Government believes that Syria has used chemical weapons on its people," or that "the NRA wants to protect the rights of gun owners." We also often ascribe legal and moral responsibility to groups. But could groups literally be intentional agents? Do they have intentions and act on the basis of their beliefs? If so, should groups be held morally responsible? Such questions are of vital importance to our understanding of the social world, and these are the questions that motivate this book.

There are those who would argue that the answer to these questions is obviously "no." For these philosophers, a book on group agency would consist in a listing of all the arguments against group agency. I haven't written such a book. It isn't obvious to me that the answer to the questions is "no," and I find the possibility of a "yes" intriguing. I have chosen, therefore, to focus on recent attempts to argue for group agency and group responsibility. I see how far these accounts can go and in the end offer an alternative approach to the issues of group agency and responsibility. This approach inevitably leaves out a vast number of theories and thinkers who have contributed to the debate. It also inevitably sets aside certain positions without a thorough and detailed argument. My aim is to provide an introductory text for those interested in current debates on group agency while also introducing a novel approach. To this end, in addition to references throughout the main text, I have included further reading lists at the end of each chapter. What I have sacrificed in terms of detail and rigor has, I hope, resulted in a readable and thought-provoking book – one that leads my reader to delve deeper into the current debates.

This book could not have been written without the encouragement and support of the Polity Press staff, especially Pascal Porcheron and Emma Hutchinson. I am grateful to the referees who offered substantial comments on its content and structure. In addition, I would like to thank Stephan Blatti, Olle Blomberg, Margaret Gilbert, Bryce Huebner, and Somogy Varga. Each took the time to read drafts and provided me with helpful comments. A special debt is owed to Tailer Ransom and Kevin Ryan, who helped proofread, construct the index, and get the references in order. Thanks are due to all of the teachers, students, friends, family, and colleagues who have helped me think through these issues over the years. I wish I had the space to acknowledge them all individually. Some of the ideas here are drawn from previous published work. I would like to express my gratitude to the *Journal of the Philosophy of Social Science*, the *Journal of Social Philosophy*, *Philosophical Explorations*, and *Cognitive Systems Research* for their permission to use my work here. Finally, I would like to thank my husband and my children, whose love and encouragement sustain me.

To Mom and Dad
For your gifts of mind and heart

Introduction

In everyday contexts we often talk as if groups were agents with attitudes such as belief and intention. Consider the following passages picked from various news outlets on an ordinary afternoon:

> In briefings earlier on Tuesday, the Israelis said they believed that the attacks March 19 involved the use of sarin gas, the same agent used in a 1995 attack in the Tokyo subway that killed 13. The Syrian attacks killed "a couple of dozens," the military official said, in what Israel judged as "a test" by President Bashar al-Assad of the international community's response. He said the government had deployed chemicals a handful of times since, but that details of those attacks were sketchier. Israel, which is in a technical state of war with Syria, has been deeply reluctant to act on its own in Syria, for fear that it could bolster President Assad by uniting anti-Israel sentiment. (Rudoren and Sanger, 2013)

> The conservatives called for the RNC to pass a resolution reaffirming its support for the 2012 platform. Among other things, the platform called for a constitutional amendment defining marriage as between a man and a woman. The committee reaffirmed its 2012 platform's "core values" on Friday, including the portion indicating that the committee believes "that marriage, the union of one man and one woman, must be upheld as the national standard." (Sullivan, 2013)

Job growth was sluggish in January for the second straight month; the government said Friday in a report likely to heighten concerns that the economy and labor market recovery may be faltering again. The report could also give the Federal Reserve second thoughts about continuing to pull back on its stimulus program aimed at holding down long-term interest rates. The Fed has begun withdrawing its bond-buying stimulus on the thinking that the economy had finally reached a sustained level of improved growth, but a series of weaker-than-expected economic data of late – including figures on car sales, manufacturing and trade – have shaken confidence. (Lee, 2014)

In addition to ascribing a belief to a group, these passages contain a host of other attributions of attitudes that we would normally describe as "mental" – as belonging to beings with a mind. Groups are said to judge, have views, thoughts and values, and even fear.

Our practice of attributing mental states and processes – such as thinking and deciding – to groups is not found simply in everyday contexts. It is also found in the context of social scientific research. As Georg Theiner and Timothy O'Connor note in their comprehensive overview of group cognition (2010), economists and political scientists talk of group rationality; sociologists, historians, and anthropologists often appeal to the concept of a group's memory; social psychologists have embraced the idea of groups as information-processing units in order to understand the ways in which problems are collectively solved; organizational theorists study the ways that firms and organizations learn and remember; evolutionary theorists have introduced the notion of group selection and argued that groups evolve into cognitive units that promote the survival of the group; zoologists and biologists posit group decision-making mechanisms in order to explain the behavior of hives, swarms, and schooling fish; and the idea of distributive cognition has been used to study small task groups such as navigation teams.

What are we to make of this practice? Are groups agents like us? Do they act on the basis of reasons, judge, deliberate? Do they have minds? And, if they do have minds, can they be held morally responsible? These are the questions that motivate this book. These are not new questions. The nature of social groups, their relation to the individuals within them, and whether they constitute a form of agency that is distinct from individual human agency have been issues consuming the minds of philosophers for centuries. This book introduces readers to recent attempts to establish that groups are intentional agents and can be held morally responsible. It also introduces readers to the substantial objections that have been raised to these accounts.

What sorts of groups are potential agents? A basic distinction is that between aggregative groups (for instance, a collection of all red-haired women) and those that have a structure and a decision-making process – what I shall call *corporate* groups. It is the latter type of group that will be my focus. The paradigm case of a corporate group is a corporation, but governments, educational institutions, or research teams will also count as corporate groups insofar as they have a structure and a decision-making process. The corporate group need not be large. A standing committee that maintains its identity despite a change in membership and that engages in decision-making will qualify as a corporate group. The word "corporate" means united or bound into one. A central question in much of the literature on group agency is how and to what extent a group of individual subjects could be united in such a way as to form a unified subject – a corporate entity. For ease I will simply use the term "group" to refer to corporate groups.

It will be helpful here to distinguish the issue of group agency from another related issue – shared agency. Shared agency refers to the ability of individuals to engage in joint actions such as moving a table together, painting a house together, or playing a game of chess. Many philosophers working on this issue believe that, in order to understand joint actions, we need to understand the ways in which individual agents share intentions. We will discuss accounts of shared intention and how they might relate to the issue of group agency in chapter 2.

Now one might object to this investigation at the outset on the grounds that groups do not exist. If they do not exist we cannot even raise the issue of whether they are agents. This objection is often motivated by a commitment to ontological individualism. Ontology refers to the study of what reality *is*, what *exists*. According to the ontological individualist, groups are composed of individual human beings and do not exist as entities "over and above" these individuals. Most theorists agree with ontological individualism, and I am no exception. Groups are composed of individuals and they act via the actions of individuals. But this doesn't support the idea that groups don't exist. Human beings are composed of cells and are nothing "over and above" their physical make-up, but this doesn't mean they don't exist. Rodin's *The Thinker* is composed of bronze, but we don't thereby say that it doesn't exist. Likewise, just because groups are *composed* of individuals and do not exist "over and above" their members does not mean they do not exist.

The real question is not whether groups exist but how we should explain group actions and properties and whether social phenomena require appeal to group properties, group actions, and group attitudes for their explanation. Methodological individualism is the view that groups and their actions can be explained solely in terms of the psychological states and processes of group members and the relations between them. Unlike its ontological sister, methodological individualism is hotly contested. Methodological collectivism argues that there are irreducible group-level properties and processes which need to play a role in the explanation of group phenomena. This book weighs in on the side of methodological collectivism by arguing for the controversial view that certain groups are genuine intentional agents that can be held accountable for their actions.

The book is organized in the following way. In chapter 1 I survey some accounts of group belief. The starting point for many of these accounts is our practice of ascribing beliefs to groups, and the aim of the accounts is to provide the conditions under which such ascriptions are true. I focus, in particular, on the work of Margaret Gilbert and Raimo Tuomela, whose writings on group belief and other group mental states form the foundation for a growing area of research called *collective intentionality*. Although current accounts offer us a number of insights, we are left wondering why group belief should be considered a species of belief at all.

In chapter 2 I turn to the issue of group intention. The literature on group intention is motivated, in part, by the phenomenon of joint action. According to many theorists, joint action requires for its explanation shared intentions or "we-intentions." The issue of whether a group can be the bearer of an intention is touched upon only indirectly, as something to be avoided. Whatever intentions are had or shared are in the heads of individuals. This is particularly clear in the work of Michael Bratman and John Searle. Nonetheless, their accounts of shared/joint intention are extremely important in the field of group intentionality and will provide us with some understanding of the reasons for wanting to ascribe an intention to a group at all.

Our discussion of theories of group belief and group intention will highlight an ambiguity in the literature. Some philosophers are interested in explaining the ways that individuals can share intentional states such as belief and intention. These accounts, then, serve as a foundation for a theory of shared agency (Bratman, 2014). Other philosophers are interested in group agency, the ability of a group *itself* to engage in purposeful action. Although group agency may involve shared agency, there is more to group agency than shared agency. When two people take a walk together they are engaged in a form of shared agency, but in doing so they do not form a unified agent to which we attribute beliefs, goals, and intentions. The connection between group agency and shared agency is not always clear in the literature. It is one of my aims here to introduce some clarity.

In chapter 3 I consider the issue of group agency directly. I consider two of the most well-defended accounts of group agency on offer and the objections that have been raised to those theories. If we are to settle the question of whether groups can have mental states and thus be intentional and moral agents, we need ask some prior questions: What are intentional agents and what are mental states? Like the theories of group belief and group intention we surveyed in chapters 1 and 2, these accounts don't really address the issue of how groups could have mental states such as belief and intention and how groups could engage in the sorts of cognitive processes that are characteristic of intentional agency (for instance, decision-making and memory). This seems to be the crux of the issue. In chapter 4 I turn, then, to theories of mental states and cognition in the philosophy of mind and consider recent attempts to extend a functionalist theory of mind to groups. Research on distributed cognition suggests that models of human cognition can be applied to groups and that doing so is explanatorily powerful.

The approaches surveyed in chapters 3 and 4 start from a theory of mind and intentional agency and see how groups might meet the criteria laid out by these theories. In chapter 5 I develop an alternative approach by suggesting that we start with our practice of making sense of others and seeing what sorts of assumptions have to be in place in order for this practice to be successful. This approach allows us to make sure that our theory of intentional agency is grounded in practice. Our practice reveals that mental states such as belief and intention are not internal states of a system or agent, as the functionalist would have it, but are states of whole systems. When I attribute a belief to an individual, I attribute it not to their head or brain but to the whole person. I argue that, if we view mental states as dispositional states of systems rather than internal states of systems, we can make sense of how groups can have mental states. Further, if we embed this dispositionalism within an explanatory theory called interpretivism, we get a more powerful explanation of our practice of making sense of others, both groups and individuals, than that offered by the functionalist approaches surveyed in chapters 3 and 4.

If certain groups can be intentional agents, the natural question to ask is whether groups can be moral agents. But that certain groups exhibit features of intentional agency is not enough to establish that they can be held morally responsible. Animals and young children are intentional agents, but they are not held morally responsible. In chapter 6 I consider recent attempts to establish that certain groups are morally responsible. I argue that, although groups may not meet the conditions for the sort of moral responsibility we find in adult human beings, they can be held *accountable* for their actions.

A philosophy professor of mine once said that philosophers are like defense lawyers. Instead of defending people they defend ideas. This book is an attempt to defend the idea of group agency. I have taken on a very difficult client. I suspect some readers will find that I haven't made my case but, in defending the idea, I hope to have shed light on the nature of agency, mind, and moral responsibility. Groups, like animals, robots, aliens, and earthworms, can be useful heuristics for thinking about what, if anything, makes human agency unique. If I have failed to persuade you of the strength of my client's case, I hope you will have seen the utility of trying to make it.

1
Group Belief

This chapter surveys recent attempts to answer the specific question of whether groups have beliefs. The accounts on offer are attempts to identify what is going on "inside" the group, or among and between individuals in the group, in order for our ascriptions of belief to the group to be true. Whatever the merits of these accounts, a pressing question remains: What is it about the phenomenon in question that makes it a case of belief?

1   Defining Belief

Before we move on to consider these accounts, it might be helpful to say a bit more about the concept of a belief. There are various theories of what a belief is, and I will discuss many of these in chapter 4 when I turn to the philosophy of mind and the nature of cognition and mental states. Some of these views, such as the view that beliefs are brain states, seem to preclude the idea that groups can be believers. There are, however, some general things we can say here that are accepted by philosophers regardless of their views about the nature of belief.

Beliefs are propositional attitudes. Consider the following belief ascribed to my son Finn. Finn believes that hamburgers are served for dinner every Friday night. In believing this, my son takes a certain attitude, the attitude of believing, toward a proposition – the proposition "Hamburgers are served for dinner every Friday night." Now he could take a different attitude toward this proposition. He could, for instance, *hope* that hamburgers are served for dinner every night (indeed, he does take this very attitude). Or he could retain the same attitude but direct it toward a different proposition. He probably has all sorts of other beliefs involving hamburgers. He believes, for instance, that hamburgers are the best food in the world and that they should be served for breakfast, lunch, and dinner. Finn's sister also has attitudes towards propositions about hamburgers. Anya fears that "Hamburgers are served for dinner every Friday night." I intend that "Hamburgers be served on Finn's birthday."

This foray into the minds of my children highlights the following: propositional attitudes involve a subject, a content (or proposition), and an attitude (belief, intention, fear, hope). In the examples above, the subjects were Finn, Anya, and me. The content of the attitudes that Finn, Anya, and I have are captured by propositions such as "Hamburgers are served for dinner every Friday night." The attitudes are those of belief, intention, or fear.

Beliefs have truth conditions – conditions under which the belief is true or false. Finn's belief that hamburgers will be served every Friday for dinner is false (much to his dismay). His belief that hamburgers are made (largely) of ground meat is true. Intentions, on the other hand, have success conditions. Although it may be true that I have the intention of serving hamburgers for Finn's birthday, my intention in itself is neither true nor false; rather, it is satisfied or unsatisfied depending on whether I succeed in serving hamburgers on Finn's birthday.

Belief is thought to be a unique attitude in that it conforms to the world, or tries to conform to the world. When we believe something truly, our mind conforms to the world. Our belief matches the state of affairs out in the world. False beliefs, though they fail to do so, attempt to conform to the world. Intentions, on the other hand, aim at getting the world to fit with our mind. My intention to make hamburgers for Finn's birthday is satisfied or fulfilled only when the world (with me in it) conforms to that intention. Intentions have what John Searle calls a world-to-mind direction of fit, whereas beliefs have a mind-to-world direction of fit (Searle, 1983).

This is where the consensus on the nature of belief ends. Debates rage about the subject of propositional attitudes. For instance, philosophers debate whether animals have propositional attitudes. There are also debates about the nature of belief. Some philosophers argue, for instance, that beliefs are brain states, others that beliefs are functional states to be defined in terms of the role they play and that these roles could be realized by other things besides brains (computers, for instance), and yet others that beliefs are best thought of as social statuses which make sense only against the backdrop of various social practices. Finally, there are debates about the content of propositional attitudes. Some philosophers think that the content is determined by factors internal to the subject, and others that the content is determined by factors external to the subject.

Philosophers writing on group belief haven't really concerned themselves with these debates in the philosophy of mind. This is partly because many have adopted methodological individualism and think that group belief ascriptions can be explained in terms of individuals' beliefs (or some other attitude), and they have left the nature of individual belief to philosophers of mind. In what follows, we will consider three accounts of the nature of group belief – the summative account, the acceptance account, and the commitment account. We will return to the nature of belief at the end of the chapter, where I will suggest some reasons for thinking that those interested in group belief ought to look more closely at debates in the philosophy of mind concerning the nature of mental states.

2   Some Recent Accounts of Group Belief

(a)   Summative Accounts

According to the summative view of group belief ascriptions, when we attribute a belief to a group we are really just saying that all or most of the group members believe this. The truth of these ascriptions, then, rests on whether or not all or most of the members believe whatever we have attributed to the group. This is the view espoused by Anthony Quinton in "Social objects" (1976):

> To ascribe mental predicates to a group is always an indirect way of ascribing such predicates to its members. With such mental states as belief and attitudes, the ascriptions are of what I have called a summative kind. To say that the industrial working class is determined to resist anti-trade union laws is to say that all or most industrial workers are so minded. (1976, p. 17)

We might formalize the summative account in the following way, where "p" stand for a proposition:

> Group G believes that p if and only if all or most of the members of G believe that p.

For instance, consider the following attribution made in the context of a department meeting: "The Assessment Committee believes that our students are able to identify patterns of valid and fallacious reasoning." According to the summative view, in order for this attribution to be true, all or most of the members of the committee must believe that the students in the program are able to identify patterns of valid and fallacious reasoning. But imagine a case where each individual believes that p but no member knows that other members have such a belief. Perhaps each person keeps it a secret that they believe that p. Would it be appropriate in this case to attribute a group belief? These sorts of cases have suggested that the summative account needs to be augmented with a condition that specifies that members know of the existence of others' beliefs. In technical terms, there must be "common knowledge" among the members. The notion of common knowledge has been analyzed in a variety of ways, and we don't have space here to peruse all of its variations.[1] The idea is that members of the group must be aware that the belief is shared and that this awareness itself is manifest to all. If we add common knowledge to the summative account, then we have something like the following:

> Group G believes that p if and only if all or most of the members of G believe that p, under conditions of common knowledge.

Now there are certain cases that the summative account seems to fit. Consider the following ascription:

> Americans believe that Mojitos are delicious.

Such an ascription is purely distributive. That is, it aims to distribute the belief that Mojitos are delicious to all or most Americans. The summative account seems to make sense of this sort of ascription quite well. But there are other cases where ascriptions are non-distributive. The belief is attributed to the group as a whole. Attributions of beliefs to groups such as committees, boards, corporations, and teams are often such cases.

There are a number of reasons to be skeptical about the adequacy of summative accounts to handle these sorts of ascriptions. For one, it seems a bit too strong to require that all or most of the members of a group believe that p in order for there to be a group belief that p (or for our ascription of a group belief to be true). Imagine a hiring committee of ten people that issues the following statement through its committee chair:

> We believe candidate X is the most qualified candidate.

Suppose only two members believe that candidate X is the most qualified. The rest of the committee either doesn't believe it or doesn't have a view of the matter at all – perhaps they didn't do any work and just went along with whatever candidate the two diligent committee members supported. All the committee's actions up to that point and going forward suggest that it believes candidate X to be the best candidate, and yet not all of the members believe this to be so. Therefore, requiring that most or all of the members believe something in order for group belief ascriptions to be true seems too strong.

Could a group believe that p if no member of the group believed that p? Intuitions are not as strong here. Many people would reject the idea that a group believes that p even in cases where no member of the group believes it. At least someone in the group has to believe it. Let's consider an example by returning to one of the passages with which I began the introduction:

> The conservatives called for the RNC to pass a resolution reaffirming its support for the 2012 platform. Among other things, the platform called for a constitutional amendment defining marriage as between a man and a woman. The committee reaffirmed its 2012 platform's "core values" on Friday, including the portion indicating that the committee believes "that marriage, the union of one man and one woman, must be upheld as the national standard." (Sullivan, 2013)

In this passage a conservative committee is attributed the belief that marriage, as the union of one man and one woman, must be upheld as the national standard. Suppose we found out that no member of this committee actually believes that heterosexual marriage must be upheld as the national standard. We can suppose that some of them believe the opposite but are afraid to lose their position in the party and that some of them believe that heterosexual marriage should be the standard in their own lives but don't believe it should be the national standard. If we found this out, would we claim that the attribution is false? Would we insist that the conservative committee does not believe that heterosexual marriage must be upheld as the national standard?

It seems to me that the question of whether the committee believes this or not depends a great deal (but perhaps not exclusively) on how the committee acts and what it does. Suppose, despite the individual members' personal beliefs, the committee continues to issue statements that express and reaffirm this "core value." Members make decisions and deliberate on the basis of this core value. For instance, the committee declines to offer financial support to organizations not committed to this core value. It adds the core value to policy statements, implements education policies around it, and, when in public, members affirm that heterosexual marriage should be upheld as the national standard. Given this sort of situation, it isn't at all clear that we would resist attributing the belief to the group. Such an attribution makes sense of the way the group behaves. Now one might balk at such an example and insist that the group will behave this way precisely because at least one person believes the proposition attributed to the group, and he or she is perhaps pulling the strings. This may in fact happen, but the point of the example is to show that it is conceptually possible for there to be a case where no individual believes that p but the attribution of a group belief that p is appropriate.

But even if we insist that at least one member must believe that p in order for the group to believe that p, summative accounts fail to provide sufficient conditions for group belief. Margaret Gilbert provides the following example to motivate this criticism:

> Assume there are two committees – say, the Library Committee and the Food Committee of a residential college – with the same members. It seems quite possible to say, without contradiction, that (a) most members of the Library Committee personally believe that college members have to consume too much starch, and this is common knowledge within the Library Committee; (b) the same goes, mutatis mutandis, for the members of the Food Committee; (c) the Food Committee believes that college members have to consume too much starch, whereas the Library Committee has no opinion on the matter. It seems that one can infer that according to our intuitive conceptions it is not logically sufficient for a group belief that p either that most group members believe that p, or that there be common knowledge within the group that most members believe that p. (Gilbert, 1996, pp. 199–200)

Summative accounts, even those that require that members know of each other's beliefs, don't quite capture what is going on in many cases of group belief ascription. In many cases, when we attribute beliefs to a group, we don't want to note simply that most members have the belief in common but that the belief plays a role within the life of the group, within its deliberations, for instance. Consider a case in which every member of the philosophy department believes that smoking causes cancer. This belief is held in common, and it may even be that each faculty member believes that every other faculty member believes that smoking causes cancer. It would be unusual, however, to ascribe such a belief to the department.

The belief plays no role in the life of the department as a group – it does not enter deliberations or planning, and it doesn't influence the actions of the department or the actions of the faculty *qua* faculty. Attributions of group belief aim, in many cases, to capture the epistemic and practical concerns of the group in question and to explain the behavior of the group.

(b) Acceptance Accounts

The summative account, then, doesn't really provide us with an account of group belief at all. It provides us with an account of shared belief or commonly held belief. It doesn't, however, help us to understand our practice of attributing beliefs to groups in a non-distributive way. Acceptance accounts attempt to provide an account of group belief in terms of individual members' acceptance of a proposition. There are several acceptance accounts in the literature (Wray 2001; Hakli 2007), but my focus here will be on the work of Raimo Tuomela, who identifies a number of different varieties of group belief. I don't have space here to consider all of these accounts. Instead I'll focus on his account of group belief where the group in question is a corporate group of the sort I have identified above.

According to Tuomela, a group, such as a corporation, believes something if and only if there are members within the organization who have a special position and decision-making role and those folks accept together (or jointly accept) that proposition as the view of the group. These folks know that there is such acceptance in place by all others, and the non-operative members – the poor guys on the assembly line, for instance – tacitly accept that this proposition is the view of the group. Here is the more technical analysis Tuomela provides in 'Group beliefs' (1995):

(Belief of Group) G believes that p in the social and normative circumstances C if and only if in C there are operative members $A_1 \ldots A_m$ in G with respective positions $P_1 \ldots P_m$ such that

(1) the agents $A_1 \ldots A_m$ when they are performing their social tasks in their positions $P_1 \ldots P_m$, and due to their

exercising the relevant authority system in G, (intentionally) jointly accept p as the view of G, and because of this exercise of the authority system they ought to continue to accept or positionally believe that p;

(2)   there is a mutual belief among the operative members to the effect that (1);

(3)   because of (1) the full-fledged and adequately informed non-operative members of G tend to tacitly accept – or at least ought to accept – p as members of G;

(4)   there is a mutual belief in G to the effect that (3). (1995, p. 295)

This account relies heavily on a distinction between operative and non-operative members, acceptance and belief, and the notion of correct social and normative circumstances. Let's consider each of these features in turn.

Operative members are those members who are responsible for the group belief having the content that it does. In the case of a corporation, the board of directors may be the operative members, whereas those who work on the assembly line or in the credit department, for instance, are non-operative members. Which members are operative is determined by the rules and regulations of the corporation. Such rules and regulations are part of the social and normative circumstances referred to in Tuomela's analysis.

The relevant social and normative circumstances involve tasks, social roles, and rules – either formal (resembling laws or statutes) or informal (based on informal group agreements). So, for instance, corporations have certain rules that define the roles and tasks of its members. The rules are formal in some cases and are to be found in the corporate handbook or charter. They often specify which members are operative and define the relation between operative members and non-operative members. In addition, they make clear the chain of authority and decision-making procedures.

Summative accounts require that all or some of the members believe that p in order for the group to believe that p. As we have seen, this seems too strong. Tuomela attempts to avoid this problem by requiring that operative members merely accept that p. No member actually has to believe that p. The operative members have what Tuomela calls "positional beliefs." Positional beliefs are views a position-holder has accepted as a basis for his performance of certain kinds of social tasks and are different from personal beliefs. For instance, the CEO might personally believe that it is wrong for the company to fire 10,000 employees, yet he accepts this proposition and acts on it given the fact that he holds a position of authority in the company. Positional views, then, need not be truth-related. We may accept false beliefs and therefore adopt positional views that we know to be false.

Tuomela's account has a number of merits. First, it avoids the pitfalls of the summative account. We have a theory of how the ascription to a group could be true rather than merely an account of commonly held beliefs and how it could be true even if many of the members don't actually hold the belief ascribed to the group. Second, it takes into account the fact that in certain groups there are various roles, rules, and responsibilities. Not every group member will play a role in realizing the group's belief.

There are, however, a number of concerns one might raise. First, consider, again, condition (1) of Tuomela's analysis.

(1) The agents A1 ... Am when they are performing their social tasks in their positions P1 ... Pm, and due to their exercising the relevant authority system in G, (intentionally) jointly accept p as the view of G, and because of this exercise of the authority system they ought to continue to accept or positionally believe that p.

The operative members must intentionally jointly accept p as the view of the group, where joint acceptance simply means that each operative member accepts p as the view of the group and it is common knowledge that each operative member does so. But what are we to make of the reference to "the view of the group"? *Prima facie*, what it is to have a view on some issue is to have an opinion or a belief. The "view" of the group, then, seems to be simply the belief of the group. If so, one of the necessary and sufficient conditions for group belief appears to make reference to the notion of a group belief. Tuomela's analysis appears to be circular. For Tuomela, there is a group belief that p if and only if operative members accept p as the group belief. But group belief (the view of the group rather than the view of its individual members) is the concept the analysis is supposed to illuminate by providing necessary and sufficient conditions for its application. Tuomela may have provided an account of how group beliefs are formed but he hasn't really told us what a group view or belief is.

Second, Tuomela's account opens the door to eliminativism about group belief. On his account, group belief is merely joint acceptance of a proposition. Why talk of group beliefs at all? This is an unhappy result, especially when we are confronted with our practice of epistemically appraising groups. We attribute knowledge and belief to groups in the context of epistemic and moral appraisal. But such appraisal presupposes belief. Consider the case of lying. When we accuse another person of lying to us, we accuse the person of misrepresenting the facts – facts they themselves believe to be otherwise. If my husband tells me that there isn't any chocolate ice cream left but I find some in the freezer, I will only accuse him of lying to me if I also have reason to believe that he knew it was in the freezer or believed it to be. If he didn't know or didn't believe it was in the freezer (perhaps he missed it upon inspection), then he would have misled me but he wouldn't have lied to me. Lying presupposes belief.

On December 15, 1953, tobacco executives met at the Plaza Hotel in Washington, DC, to discuss what they considered to be a crisis: research linking smoking and cancer. In less than two weeks the industry released an advertisement that appeared in newspapers across the United States entitled "A Frank Statement to Cigarette Smokers." The advertisement claimed that there was no evidence linking cigarette smoking and cancer and that the industry believed that there was no reason to think that tobacco products were harmful to one's health. That meeting, according to lawsuits filed in federal and state courts across the United States, began a decades-long campaign to deceive the public about the health risks of smoking. The tobacco industry lied. It believed that smoking causes health problems and yet it tried to persuade us otherwise. It didn't just accept this for the sake of argument. But, on Tuomela's view, it could be possible for no one in the industry or the industry itself to believe that cigarettes caused cancer. But without belief there is no lie.

(c) Commitment Accounts

According to commitment accounts, there is a sort of normativity involved in group belief (and other group attitudes such as group intention) that needs to be captured and isn't captured by the summative or acceptance views.

Consider a program assessment committee tasked with coming up with a way to assess the logical thinking skills of the department's philosophy majors. It meets to discuss the options and decides to implement the California Critical Thinking skills test. The committee tells the Chair of the department (through its committee Chair), "We believe this is the best method of assessment available to us at this time." Now suppose that one of the committee members, Professor Troublemaker, says during a department meeting, "The California Critical Thinking Skills test is a farce. My two-year-old could pass it." The members of the committee and the Chair of the department are likely to respond in a less than positive way. They might say to Professor Troublemaker, "We agreed that it was the best method! Why are you doing this?"

According to Margaret Gilbert (1994), a "shocked rebuke" will be a very normal and appropriate response to this sort of behavior. Gilbert argues that her account of group belief best accounts for this phenomenon. It is because there was a commitment, of a sort, that bound the committee members together that such a response is appropriate. The obligations and entitlements that arise from this commitment justify the shocked rebuke. The commitment is of a very special kind, however. According to Gilbert, who calls this a *joint commitment*, paradigmatic social groups are constituted by one or more joint commitments. When they are so constituted they become "plural subjects," to which actions and intentional states may be ascribed.

In the case of belief, groups become the plural subject of a belief by forming a joint commitment to believe as a body. What is a joint commitment and what does it mean to "believe as a body"? Let's take each of these questions in turn.

In recent work (2013) Gilbert highlights the distinction between a personal commitment and a joint commitment. Personal commitments are commitments we can make by ourselves and can rescind on our own. These commitments have a certain normative force. When I decide to write a book I have a reason to pursue certain courses of action rather than others, and if I fail to pursue actions conducive to writing a book I could be charged with irrationality if there are no overriding reasons that would explain my choice of action. I can, however, rescind my decision to write a book. I have that discretion.

Joint commitments are commitments made by two or more people and cannot be rescinded unilaterally. Just as individual decisions do, joint commitments rationalize action. When one becomes party to a joint commitment it gives one reason to act in a certain way, and if one doesn't one is susceptible to charges of irrationality and, in addition, rebuke from other parties. Consider again the program assessment committee and the following attribution of belief to that group: the committee believes that the California Critical Thinking Skills test is a valid assessment tool. If this attribution is true of this group it is, according to Gilbert, because they have formed a joint commitment that binds them to certain courses of action. If Professor Troublemaker says something opposite the group's belief, then the others are justified in rebuking her. Professor Troublemaker can't just change the group belief on her own. Their joint commitment brings with it certain obligations and entitlements. The obligations involved in joint commitments are not, according to Gilbert, moral obligations but a function of the fact that the parties have together imposed rationally constraining commitments on each other. As a direct result of this, each member is now in a position to call any one of the other members to order. Like personal commitments, joint commitments involve the norms of practical rationality.

If personal commitments are formed by an act of the personal will, how are joint commitments formed? According to Gilbert, they are formed when each individual expresses their readiness or willingness jointly to commit them all to X as a body (again where X stands for an action or mental state) under conditions of common knowledge. This set of expressions of readiness suffices jointly to commit them all, and the relevant obligations and entitlements then come into play. The expression of readiness need not be explicit. Simply nodding one's head or failing to object to a course of action might, in the right context, constitute expressing one's willingness. The members of the program assessment committee need not have all said, "I express my willingness to commit to believing as a body that the California Critical Thinking Skills test is a suitable assessment tool." The fact that no one objected strongly to its use can, according to Gilbert, constitute a readiness to be jointly committed with the others.

Once a joint commitment is formed, each individual is committed (though not via a personal commitment) to doing certain things. At this point we can return to the notion of believing as a body. Recall that, in a case of group belief, members jointly commit to believe that p as a body. What does it mean to believe as a body? This is the way Gilbert puts it: "The members are jointly committed to emulate, by virtue of their combined actions and utterances, a single believer of the proposition in question" (2013, p. 213).

Gilbert makes it clear that members themselves do not have to believe that p in order to achieve this. This allows her to avoid the pitfalls of the summative accounts. Neither do the members have to act as if they personally believe that p. Doing one's part in the context of a group belief, then, seems to involve at least not saying anything contrary to the group belief while speaking as a member of the group or acting contrary to the group belief while acting in one's capacity as a group member. One who participates in a joint commitment to believe that p thereby accepts an obligation to do what he can to bring it about that any joint endeavors among the members of S be conducted on the assumption that p is true. He is entitled to expect others' support in bringing this about. Further, if one does believe something that is inconsistent with p, one is required at least not to express that belief baldly. The committee members would have a right to rebuke one of their own if, in acting as a member of the committee, that person expressed views that were contrary to the group view without prefacing their remarks by stating, "I personally believe that ... "

One might wonder at this point what the difference is between Tuomela's acceptance account and Gilbert's commitment account. On the face of it, expressing one's willingness or readiness to be jointly committed to believing as a body that p looks very close to accepting p as the view of the group, which is basically the acceptance account. Indeed, in early work on this topic (1987, 1989), Gilbert describes the parties to a group belief as "jointly accepting" the relevant proposition. For Gilbert, however, the expression of willingness to be jointly committed is a precursor to the setting up of a pool of wills. Once each member expresses his or her willingness, something new comes into being – a joint commitment. Unlike the acceptance view, Gilbert's joint commitment view does not reduce to an individual commitment or acceptance. Whatever the individuals are committed to in a joint commitment is derivative of the joint commitment. This allows Gilbert to avoid worries about eliminativism that plague Tuomela's account. We cannot eliminate the notion of joint commitment because it cannot be reduced to individual commitments or acceptances. In addition, the notion of acceptance does not provide the normativity Gilbert thinks is part and parcel of the social world. It is from the joint commitment that obligations and entitlements flow, and this is unique to her account.

The framework of joint commitment has been used by Gilbert to explain not just group belief but also a wide range of social phenomena. As we shall see in chapter 2, Gilbert offers a joint commitment account of group intention as well. Critics of her account have raised a number of concerns. Consider, again, our tobacco company. Is it necessary that each member of the tobacco company express their willingness to be jointly committed? This seems too demanding. Gilbert's theory is developed with dyads and small committees in mind. But it doesn't seem to fit large-scale groups such as corporations, where members often leave but both the organization and its beliefs remain the same. On Gilbert's account, members must intentionally express their willingness to be jointly committed with the others. However, in larger groups or groups that do not engage in a joint discussion about the group's view but hold a vote, one that is private so that members cannot know how the others voted, there is no way to know the intentions of the other participants (Baltzer, 2002). Gilbert has responded to this criticism by saying that her account provides the core notion of a group belief. Other cases of group belief will be extensions of this core. The beliefs of large-scale groups or corporations, for instance, can be explained by members allowing certain people to form the group's beliefs – a prior joint commitment to allow certain members to form, via further joint commitments, the group's beliefs.

Gilbert's appeal to an irreducible normative element has also been criticized. Critics (Bratman 2007, 2014; Bittner 2002) have argued that she introduces an apparatus to explain a type of normativity that either isn't there or doesn't need to be explained by a new apparatus. Why appeal to a technical notion such as joint commitment when one could appeal to a general principle of fidelity? A principle of fidelity such as "Do what you say you will do" will ensure that, once each individual expresses their willingness to act as a body, various expectations and obligations will be set up. Consider again the assessment committee. Professor Troublemaker might best be understood as violating Gricean norms of conversation. He has said something that could be seen as uncooperative, since he has not made his conversational contribution "by the accepted purpose or direction of the talk exchange in which you are engaged" (Grice, 1975). Professor Troublemaker is going in the wrong direction! If the norms involved in these cases can be understood in terms of conversational norms, then why introduce a new apparatus to do so?[2]

One of the merits of Gilbert's account is that it seems to acknowledge groups as the bearer of mental states. This fits well with our practice of attributing beliefs to groups. But according to some critics (Velleman, 1997) Gilbert's account doesn't go far enough to explain how plural subjects are subjects, and we might second that by saying that she doesn't show how group belief is really a species of belief. She argues that the notion of a joint commitment is a primitive one and that members of a group will have an intuitive idea of what it is to be jointly committed to believing as a group, but what we want from a theory of group belief is an account of why group belief is *belief-like*. As with Tuomela's acceptance account, we seem to have an account of how group beliefs are realized or formed (via joint commitments) but no account of why group beliefs should be counted as beliefs at all.

Gilbert hasn't remained entirely silent on this issue. On the analogy between individual and group belief she writes:

Let me now say a word more on the analogy between group beliefs and the beliefs of individuals. Both of these "phenomena of belief" may be seen as essentially involving a relation between a proposition and a subject ... The proposition figures in the life of the group or in the life of the individual. In picking out belief, then, we may not primarily be concerned to pick out a special state of mind, so much as picking out a certain proposition as one which has an explanatory role to play in an account of the behavior of individuals on the one hand and sets of individuals on the other ... If we look at things this way the analogy between group belief and individual belief may seem, after all, to be quite close. (1989, p. 313)

It is this very insight that motivates my own positive proposal, developed in chapter 5, for understanding group attitudes and agency.

3   Taking Stock

Summative accounts of group belief attempt to identify the group's belief with the members' beliefs. This has seemed insufficient to capture the various ways in which we want to talk about the belief of a group. Tuomela and Gilbert have provided accounts that identify the phenomenon with a set of complex individual attitudes and the relations between them. Some of the criticisms raised against these accounts focus on the problem of providing a unified theory – a single account that applies to lots of different types of groups and that explains various aspects of our practice of attributing beliefs to groups. Each theory seems capable of handling some phenomena, but not all. Summative accounts seem to explain attributions that are made in a distributive fashion. In this respect they are not accounts of group belief at all but accounts of commonly held or shared beliefs. Of the accounts that do provide analyses of group belief, Tuomela's seems to handle the case of larger organizations such as corporations. Gilbert's account seems to be best suited to small, intimate groups, such as committees, or even dyads. Group beliefs seem to be realized in different ways by different groups. But if this is the case, the search for a single analysis of group belief (or of the core notion of group belief) seems misplaced. Perhaps Gilbert's and Tuomela's accounts are not competitors but two ways in which certain groups come to realize their beliefs.

In addition, Gilbert and Tuomela's accounts seem to suggest that it is possible for a group to have just one belief. But, in order to have a belief, a subject must have lots of other beliefs (Davidson, 1975). If I believe that it is raining outside I am able to do so because I also have beliefs about the distinction between inside and outside, rain, and weather. Beliefs are attributed only against the backdrop of a web of other beliefs. It isn't possible for an agent to have just one belief. If we want to understand not simply how group beliefs are formed but also why group belief is a species of belief, we need to consider the nature of belief and intentional agency more broadly.

4   Suggestions for Further Reading

Raimo Tuomela and Margaret Gilbert's work on group belief is by far the most influential. Their recent books (Gilbert, 2013; Tuomela, 2013) will provide the reader with a deeper understanding of their approach. Those who want to hear more about the acceptance view should read Raul Hakli (2007) and, for the view that group beliefs are not just acceptances, see Schmitt (2014). For an excellent discussion of the epistemic consequences of group belief, see Mathiesen (2006). For an approach that tries to understand what people mean when they ascribe beliefs to groups, see Jones (2010).

5   Discussion Questions

1   Do we attribute beliefs to groups? What sorts of groups?
2   Which account of group belief seems the most plausible to you? Why?
3   Many religious groups have a creed or a statement of faith. Is a creed a statement of group belief? What theory

of group belief makes the most sense of the belief of a religious group?

4   What, according to Gilbert and Tuomela, is the difference between shared belief and group belief?

5   Donald Davidson (1975) has argued that in order to have a belief you have to have lots of other beliefs (although he doesn't specify how many). Do you think this is correct? Could an intentional agent have a single belief?

2
Group Intention

In chapter 1 we considered various accounts of group belief. In this chapter we turn to consider group intention. Some of the accounts we considered in chapter 1 have been extended to make sense of group intention as well, so some of the philosophers and terminology will be familiar. Our discussion of group belief was motivated by reflection on our practice of ascribing beliefs. Our practice also ascribes intentions to groups. But much of the literature on group intention has been motivated not by reflection on our practice of ascribing mental states to groups but by considering the phenomenon of joint intentional action, where this refers to the ways in which people can purposefully act together.

1 Defining Intention

Intentions are what distinguish actions – things that I do – from mere happenings – things that happen to me. Tripping is something that happens to me; I don't do it on purpose or with an intention. It isn't part of my plan. If, on the other hand, I perform a prat fall, I do so with an intention or purpose. I have discretion and control over the action, and it is my intention that provides me with such discretion. In both cases my bodily movements may be the same. But in the latter case I *do* something. In the former something happens to me. As with belief, there are various debates in the philosophy of mind regarding the nature of intention. Some philosophers argue that intention is not a distinct mental state but a complex of belief and desire (Davidson, 1963), others argue that intention is not a mental state at all (Anscombe, 1957).

We engage in intentional actions all the time. Some of them are simple, such as hailing a cab. Others are more complex, such as writing a research paper. We also engage in intentional actions together with others – joint actions such as playing games, dancing the tango, singing a duet, and waging war. Such actions can be distinguished from things that we do with others in a loose sense of the word. When we drive on the street we do so with many other cars and drivers and even coordinate our actions so as to avoid running into each other, but we would not characterize ourselves as driving together. Joint actions refer to doing things together in a robust sense.

If joint actions are intentional – things that we do rather than things that happen to us – how are we to understand the intentions involved? Are they the intentions of individuals or are they the intentions of the group? Answers to these questions fall roughly into four categories: goal accounts, mode accounts, shared accounts, and commitment accounts.

2   Goal Accounts

One might object to the whole idea of group intentions and argue that joint action can be explained in terms of shared goals or group ends. This is the view espoused by Seumas Miller.[1] According to Miller (2001), joint actions are actions directed at a common or group end. A group end is an end that more than one agent has, and this end is realized by various actions of individuals. Consider a soccer team that wins a match. Winning the game is something that they do. It is an intentional action. But it does not, according to Miller, require shared or group intention, just individual intentions and group ends or goals. Each individual soccer player has the end of winning the game, and each performs various intentional actions in order to reach that goal. They do so, however, only if they also believe (truly) that the other members of the team have that goal and will contribute actions to reaching that goal. That is, each member acts on the condition that the others will act and on the condition that they have the same group end.

According to Miller, a collective end is different than an individual end in a number of respects. First, group ends are shared in a strong sense. If Finn and Anya both have the goal of eating ice cream, then they share a goal in a weak sense. These individual goals could be satisfied by multiple states of affairs. Finn might eat an ice cream on Tuesday and Anya one on Friday. By shared end, Miller means a set of individual ends that would be realized by *one single* state of affairs. If, for instance, Finn and Anya had the goal of eating ice cream together, there would be only one single state of affairs that would constitute the realization of both Anya's end of eating ice cream with Finn and Finn's goal of eating ice cream with Anya, namely the state of affairs in which they eat ice cream together.

Second, group ends are shared by virtue of being interdependent. Finn's goal to eat ice cream together depends on Anya's goal to eat ice cream together and vice versa. Each forms this goal because of the other's goal. Finally, group ends are "mutually open" to those who have them. That is, if there is a group end, those who possess it believe (truly) of each other that they have it. Finn and Anya are aware that each has the goal of eating ice cream with the other.

Critics of this approach (e.g., Bratman, 2014) stress the need for intentions to explain certain forms of shared agency. Intentions are plans that play a unique role in guiding and informing action. When I form the intention to go to the gym today, it puts in place rational constraints that govern my actions. This intention will cause me to do certain things (such as collecting my gym clothes) and avoid doing others (such as climbing back into bed). When I am faced with a choice of what to do, my intention to go to the gym will help me arbitrate between options. Intentions are sort of like commitments to ourselves. They set out a plan of action, and it is on the basis of this plan that we choose various other actions. This doesn't mean that we can't change our intentions or pursue courses of action that are inconsistent with them. I can just climb back into bed if I want to, but to do so is to court irrationality. If I truly intend to go to the gym, rationality requires that my actions are consistent with my plans. The idea is that, in many cases of joint action, we need intentions that play a similar role in guiding and informing the action of the group. Group ends won't do that because ends or goals are not rationally binding in the way that intentions are, or so the argument goes.[2]

It is also not clear how Miller's account would apply to cases of large groups. Can we explain the actions of IBM by appeal to the collective goals of each employee? This seems a bit too stringent. Maybe some of them do share similar ends or goals, but Miller's view requires knowledge that all others share these ends and that the ends are interdependent. It is not clear how this could be achieved by large groups of people who may not know each other or interact with each other directly.[3]

Finally, we do actually attribute intentions to groups. The subject, at times, seems to be the group itself rather than the individuals within the group. On Miller's account, groups themselves don't have ends or intentions. What does this mean for our practice of attributing intentions to groups? Miller could respond to this question by saying that our ascriptions are just short-handed ways of referring to collective ends and goals, and that our ascriptions are true only if there are, indeed, such collective ends present. But then it seems difficult to square this with the fact that often we don't know anything about the goals and ends of individual participants or anything about the knowledge they have of others' goals and ends. When we say that Facebook now intends to work with the US Drug Enforcement Agency (DEA), we don't know anything at all about the collective ends that individuals within the organization might be working toward. It is hard to see, then, how our ascriptions are somehow a short-handed way of referring to those complicated social relations.

Now one might reply that we are able to refer to lots of things without knowing the ultimate nature of the referent (the thing in the world to which we are trying to refer). We refer to water, for instance, using the term "water," and we did so for many, many, many, years without knowing that its ultimate nature was H_2O. The same goes for collective ends, so we can refer to collective ends using the term "group intention" without knowing their complicated nature. But there is a significant difference between the case of water and the case of collective ends. Water is a natural kind. It is something found out in the world and is there independent of our conceptions of it. This is not so with collective ends. Collective ends, if they exist, are what philosophers call social kinds. Social kinds are determined by human knowledge and perception. Their meaning and existence is not independent of our knowledge of them. If our practice of attributing intentions to groups is really just a short-handed way of referring to collective ends, then we should know that it is. Or at least it would be more obvious that this is what we are doing.

A second way Miller might respond is to say that our attributions of intention to groups are just mistaken and are always false. Perhaps he would even suggest that we replace all talk of group intentions with talk of collective ends. But why should we adopt such a drastic dismissal of our practice? Perhaps collective ends do play a role in explaining lots of aspects of the social world. But our talk of what "we intend" to do and what groups intend to do doesn't seem obviously false, and it may very well play a distinct role in understanding different aspects of the social world.

3 Mode Accounts

Reflection on how and why we do things with others has led some philosophers to focus on the fact that, when we act together with others, we seem to be acting from a different "mind set." We have the "we" in mind. We think and act in a way that keeps in mind the group of which we are a part and the reasons for which the group is acting. As Tuomela calls it, we think in the "we-mode." John Searle (1990) provides a nice example to highlight the special nature of joint intentional action. Imagine a group of people sitting on the grass enjoying a sunny afternoon in the park. Suddenly it grows dark and starts to rain. They all get up and run to a centrally located place. In this scenario each individual has the intention "I am running to shelter," and their intentions are had independently of one another. Now imagine a situation in which there is a group of actors who are performing a play. At one point in the play they perform the same actions done by the individuals in the above scenario. But now they do it as a performance. According to Searle, the latter actions involve an intention of the form "we intend to do x" – a group intention. The group intention (Searle calls it a collective intention) is different both from an individual intention of the form "I intend to do x" and from the summation of individual intentions of this form. It is also different from a group end, in that this intention plays a causal role in determining what intentions I will form as an individual.

Group intentions involve a sense of acting and willing something together. Individual intentions involved in this enterprise are derived from the group intention, according to Searle. It is precisely because there is a "we-intention" that the actors move in the various ways that they do and form individual intentions that help them to coordinate with one another.

But what is a we-intention? Is it the intention of an individual or of a group? Searle specifies that anything we say about group intention must meet the following conditions of adequacy:

1 It must be consistent with the fact that society is nothing over and above the individuals that comprise it. All consciousness and intentionality is in the minds of individuals – specifically, individual brains.
2 It must be consistent with the fact that all intentionality could be had by a brain in a vat.

Searle's first criterion of adequacy denies that groups can be the bearer of mental states. We-intentions are not the intentions of the group but are a special sort of mental state in the mind of the individual. Recall the threefold distinction we made when we discussed propositional attitudes in chapter 1 – subject, attitude, and content. The ascription "Sue believes that ice cream is tasty" has a subject – Sue –

an attitude – that of belief – and a content, "Ice cream is tasty." In "Sue intends to eat ice cream," the subject is still Sue, but the attitude has changed to an intention and the content is "Eat ice cream." According to Searle, in addition to subject, attitude, and content, there are different modes that a subject can enter. Just as we can form attitudes from the first-person perspective – the I-mode – we can also form attitudes from the we-mode and, thus, form we-intentions and even we-beliefs. Such beliefs are formed in group contexts but are not the beliefs of a group.[4] The second criterion is motivated by a certain form of content internalism. According to this condition, all intentionality is independent of what the real world is like. Radical mistake is possible. We could all be in the Matrix right now and be deceived about the nature of the world, and yet the nature of intentionality would remain the same.

Searle's account has been criticized on various grounds. Searle himself acknowledges that it is because of the special nature of group intentions that we are able to distinguish in the example above between the two cases of individuals running for cover. There is something about group intentions that coordinates individual, independent actions into a joint action. But isolated, perhaps even solipsistic, we-intentions do not, in themselves, seem to be enough to direct and coordinate the individual intentional actions of which the joint action is comprised (Meijers, 2003). Suppose, for instance, that none of the actors knew of the other actors' we-intention. It would seem to be a complete accident that they acted together. Indeed, it would seem as fortuitous as a group of individuals who just happen to get up at the same time and run for cover. In order to avoid this criticism, Searle (2010) has recently added a requirement that participants in a joint action have the belief that others have similar we-intentions.

But there are additional worries. We-intentions seem pretty mysterious. Nothing in our experience and in our everyday practice of ascribing intentions to others (and to groups) seems to confirm their existence. For instance, after seeing a soccer team win a game, I don't say of the coach that he we-intended to use his best players. We don't distinguish our own intentions in anything like Searle's terminology. Personally, I don't think I have ever had a we-intention, though I have had lots of thoughts about what *we* will do and beliefs about what *we* should do (where "we" refers to groups in my life). I just don't have any experience of changing modes – which must happen a whole lot given the complexity of social life. Searle describes the we-mode as irreducible. It is a primitive way of thinking, one that we share with animals. But saying that it is primitive doesn't make it any less mysterious.

Now Searle might respond here by saying that our everyday practice doesn't always reflect reality and that we could be wrong about the nature of our own intentions. This is true. But given the prevalence of joint actions – we do things together all the time – you would think that the we-mode would be more intuitive. Now if all that Searle means by we-mode is that individuals form intentions by considering the group's perspective, this seems non-controversial. But nothing about this requires the positing of a we-intention – a different mode of intending. I can simply intend from the first-person perspective various things about the "we" of which I am a part. As we shall see, Michael Bratman (1993, 2014) proposes such a position and, as we shall also see, the idea of being able to intend that *we* do something is controversial.

It is worth making the point here that, strictly speaking, Searle's account is not an account of *group* intentions. For Searle (and Miller as well), groups don't have intentions, only individuals do. Joint action is explained solely in terms of individual members and their intentions. Though these intentions make reference to a "we," Searle's account does not acknowledge groups as the appropriate subjects of intentional states.

Raimo Tuomela (2006) also provides an account of the intentions underlying joint actions that appeals to the notion of a we-intention. But, unlike Searle's account, we-intentions are not, on Tuomela's view, primitive. They do not resist analysis. For Tuomela, we-intentions are individual intentions to do one's part in a joint action, plus beliefs about the conditions under which the joint action can be performed and the presence of similar intentions and beliefs in the minds of others. Here is Tuomela's own formulation:

A member A_i of a group g *we-intends* to do X if and only if

(1) A_i intends to do his part of X (as his part of X);

(2) A_i has a belief to the effect that the joint action oppor-
      tunities for an intentional performance of X will obtain
      (or at least probably will obtain), especially that a right
      number of the full-fledged and adequately informed
      members of g, as required for the performance of X, will
      (or at least probably will) perform their parts of X,
      which under normal conditions will result in an inten-
      tional joint performance of X by the participants;

(3) A_i believes that there is (or will be) a mutual belief among
      the participating members of g (or at least among those
      participants who perform their parts of X intentionally
      as their parts of X there is or will be a mutual belief) to
      the effect that the joint action opportunities for an inten-
      tional performance of X will obtain (or at least probably
      will obtain);

(4)   (1) in part because of (2) and (3). (2006, p. 43)

Agents jointly intend to perform an action when each member
has the we-intention to perform X and everyone believes
everyone else also has the we-intention to perform the action.
Again, Tuomela provides the following formulation:

Agents $A_1, \ldots A_i, \ldots A_m$ have the *joint intention to perform a
joint action X* if and only if

(1)   these agents have the we-intention (or are disposed to
      form the we-intention) to perform X; and

(2)   there is a mutual belief among them to the effect that (1).
      (Ibid., p. 45)

We-intentions on Tuomela's account, then, seem less mysterious. They don't require a special mode of thinking; rather, they
involve intentions and beliefs about one's part in a group
action and beliefs about the beliefs and intentions of other
members of the group.

Tuomela, too, has his critics. For one, his analysis doesn't
seem to help explain actions that occur "on the fly," so to
speak. If all these beliefs and intentions have to be in place
for the existence of a joint intention, then it seems to require
too much for those joint actions that happen without any

prior planning (Kutz, 2000). Of course Tuomela might argue that this apparatus is tacit and need not be formed explicitly. Just as many of our actions are guided by intentions that we never explicitly form, so too joint intentions can be working tacitly within our cognitive system. Still, the complexity of Tuomela's account calls into question its psychological plausibility.

The requirement of mutual belief involves a fairly complex understanding of the concept of belief. Individuals must believe that others have beliefs. This presupposes a theory of other minds. But animals and young children surely engage in joint action, and yet empirical research suggests that they do not have a very sophisticated theory of other minds. This suggests that Tuomela's account of joint intention, the intentional structure that underlies joint action, is too sophisticated to serve as a general account of this phenomenon (Tollefsen, 2005). Because Searle appeals to a primitive capacity to we-intend, his account extends easily to animals and children and might provide a more phylogenically and ontogenetically plausible account of the basis of joint action.

We might also worry that Tuomela's account is meant to apply to small-scale groups where mutual belief is easily established. It is difficult to see how his account would extend to larger groups such as a corporation. Is it really plausible to think that every member of an organization needs to have a we-intention, of the sort Tuomela describes, in order for there to be a group action? And how could such we-intentions be formed among people who do not have access to the beliefs of other members of the group?

In recent work Tuomela (2013) offers an account of group intention that, like his account of group belief, is meant to apply to larger, more structured groups, such as organizations. It is meant to account for the way a group, as such, could be the appropriate subject of an intention. His account is very technical as it is embedded within the framework of various other notions he defines, such as shared intention, joint intention (analyzed above), and we-mode acting. Here is how he formulates his account:

> Group g intends to see to it that X obtains (or comes about, etc., where X is an action or state) as a group if and only if

there are authorized operative members or individuals for decision making in relation to g such that:

(1) Either (a) these operative agents are internally authorized and, acting as group members in the we-mode, have formed the joint intention that g through its members will see to it that X, or (b) the operative members for decision making are externally authorized to see to it that X and have been ordered by some other group members (non-operatives for decision making but operative for plan-realizing action) to actually achieve or realize X having formed the shared intention to do it;

(2) In (1) there is a respective mutual belief among the operative members to the effect that (1) (a) or (1) (b);

(3) Both (a) in the internally and (b) in the externally authorized cases the non-operative members qua members of g group normatively ought to accept as true that their group g intends to perform X (as specified in clause (1) and go along with the group's directives).

(4) There is a mutual belief in g to the effect that (3) or at least this belief should be attainable by the members. (2013, p. 87)

I can't hope to offer a detailed exegesis of this account here. But let's see if we can't say in a more straightforward way what Tuomela might be trying to capture here. As in his account of group belief, Tuomela wants to distinguish operative and non-operative members. Not all members have to intend in order for there to be a group intention. In large, structured groups such as organizations, it is the operative members that set the intentions for the group, either by forming the joint intention to do so or by being told to do so by someone external (in a corporation perhaps these are the shareholders) and sharing the intention to act as they have been told. All the operative members know both that either of these two things obtain and that all the others know. Further, the non-operative members accept that their group intends to perform X, and they all know that they know (or could know). The notions of shared intention and joint intention are technical notions here, and I don't have space to provide Tuomela's analysis of them. The basic idea is that there is some subset of the group that sets the group's intentions and the others accept it as the intention of the group.

One thing to note is that Tuomela is giving an analysis of the concept of group intention in terms of necessary and sufficient conditions. This means that, if the conditions 1 to 4 are met, this is all we need for group intention. It also means that, if these conditions are not present, we don't have a group intention. So if a corporation, for instance, fails to meet these conditions, the corporation would not have a group intention. Is it really plausible to think that this is the only way in which a corporate group could realize an intention? And how would we go about verifying it? This seems a bit too demanding and practically impossible to verify. Even if one is convinced by this analysis, we are still left wondering why this complicated set of conditions counts as a group intention. What we seem to have is an account of how group intention is realized or formed in a group. What is needed is a discussion of why group intentions should count as intentions at all.

4 Shared Accounts

As we have seen, the introduction of a different mode of thought, either a primitive mode or one analyzed in terms of individual intentions, has been thought to complicate matters. Either it introduces something mysterious or, as in Tuomela's case, it introduces layers of complexity that seem psychologically implausible. Michael Bratman (1993, 2014) attempts to explain the intentional structure of joint action without appeal to a different mode of thought. He uses the phrase "shared intention" rather than joint intention and motivates his account by reflecting on the role that shared intentions play in shaping and informing joint actions. First, shared intentions help to coordinate our intentional actions. For instance, our shared intention of washing the dishes will guide each of our intentional actions toward satisfying the goal of washing the dishes. Thus, someone will wash the dishes before rinsing them and someone will rinse them before drying them. Second, our shared intention will coordinate our actions by making sure that our own personal plans of action meld together. If I plan to do the washing, then I will check with your plan and see if there is any conflict. Third, shared intentions act as a backdrop against which bargaining and negotiation occur. Conflicts about who does the washing and who does the drying will be resolved by considering the fact that we share the intention to do the dishes. Thus, shared intention unifies and coordinates individual intentional actions by tracking the goals accepted by each individual.

Consider a case in which you and I intend to wash the dishes together. If this intention is a shared intention, then it is not a matter of your having an intention to wash the dishes and my having an intention to wash the dishes. Nor is it a matter of each of us having an atomistically conceived we-intention to wash the dishes. Such coincident intentions do not insure that each of us knows of the other's intention and that we are committed to the joint action of washing the dishes together. Further, an explicit promise made to each other does not seem to insure that we share an intention either. Because I might be lying to you and have no intention of washing the dishes with you. Thus, explicit promises are not sufficient for shared intention. Nor are they necessary for shared intention. Bratman provides an example from Hume to highlight this. "Consider Hume's example of two people in a row boat who row together 'tho they have never given promises to each other.' Such rowers may well have a shared intention to row the boat together" (Bratman, 1993, pp. 98–9).

What do shared intentions consist in, according to Bratman? Bratman shares Searle's commitment to individualism in that he does not think that shared intentions are the intentions of a group:

> To understand shared intention, then, we should not appeal to an attitude in the mind of some superagent; nor should we assume that shared intentions are always grounded in prior promises. My conjecture is that we should, instead, understand shared intention, in the basic case, as a state of affairs consisting primarily of appropriate attitudes of each individual participant and their interrelations. (1993, p. 99)

Shared intentions are not the intentions of individuals nor are they the intentions of a group. They are a state of affairs consisting of a set of interrelated individual intentional states. Here is a somewhat simplified version of Bratman's analysis of shared intention. We intend to wash the dishes if and only if:

(1) (a) I intend that we wash the dishes and (b) You intend that we wash the dishes.
(2) I intend that we wash the dishes in accordance with and because of 1a and 1b; you intend likewise.
(3) 1 and 2 are common knowledge between us. (Ibid., p. 104)

As a first approximation this complex of intentional attitudes seems plausible. But consider a case in which each of us intends to wash the dishes together and each of us does so in part because of the other's intention. However, I intend to wash the dishes with hot water and you intend to wash them with cold water. All of this is common knowledge, and we will not compromise. Is there a group intention present? It seems not. In this case we do not have our subplans coordinated in the appropriate way. Recall that one of the jobs that shared intention has is to coordinate our individual plans and goals. In the example above our individual subplans are in conflict, and this would prevent us from achieving our goal of getting the dishes washed.

Bratman avoids this counterexample by adding a clause about participants' subplans. Participants must intend that their subplans mesh with each other. This doesn't mean they have to match. If my subplan involves the intention to wash the dishes with a certain kind of soap, you intend to wash them with hot water, and I have no preference about the water temperature, then our subplans mesh even though they don't match exactly. But if we have subplans to wash the dishes with different water temperatures, our subplans do not mesh, as it would be impossible to accommodate both. Bratman reformulates the account in the following way:

We intend to J if and only if:

1 (a) I intend that we J and (b) you intend that we J
2 I intend that we J in accordance with and because of 1a and 1b, and meshing subplans of 1a and 1b, you intend the same.
3 1 and 2 are common knowledge. (1993, p. 106)

A joint action or shared intentional action, as Bratman calls it, occurs when this complex of attitudes results in our J-ing.

Our J-ing is a shared intentional activity if and only if

(A) We J.
(B) We have the attitudes specified in (1)(a) and (1)(b) and (2) and,
(C) (B) leads to (A) by way of mutual responsiveness (in the pursuit of J-ing) in intention and action.

Bratman is clear that his analysis is limited. It provides an account of a certain type of social phenomenon: "The limitation is that my focus will be primarily on the shared intentional activities of small, adult groups in the absence of asymmetric authority relations within those groups, and in which the individual who are participants remain constant over time" (2014, p. 7). We can hardly criticize his account, then, for not being able to understand our ascriptions of intention to what I have called corporate agents. Recall, corporate agents are those that remain the same despite a change of membership. Often they involve asymmetric authority relations, as in the organizational context. Bratman is offering an account of what he calls "modest sociality." He wants to use the metaphysical and normative resources of his planning agency theory (developed with the individual in mind) to explain the actions of small teams and dyads rather than those groups embedded in an institutional setting. Even this limited theory, however, has come under fire.

Bratman avoids positing a group agent by trying to explain shared intentions in terms of individual attitudes with common contents that are distinctively social in the sense that solitary individuals could not have them. As with Searle and Tuomela, there are no group intentions. But critics have argued that it is not possible for me, an individual, to have an intention of the form "I intend that we do J." This line of argument has been developed, in slightly different ways, in papers by Annette Baier (1997), Frederick Stoutland (1997), and J. David Velleman (1997). Consider Velleman's formulation of the problem as it applies to Bratman's account:

> How can I frame the intention that "we" are going to act, if I simultaneously regard the matter as being partly up to you?

> And how can I continue to regard the matter as partly up to you, if I have already decided that we really are going to act? The model seems to require the exercise of more discretion than there is to go around. (1997, p. 5)

Normally, when I intend to do something, the action I intend to do is under my control. And in normal cases of shared intention (cases where there is no coercion or where I am not in control of your actions) the other agent is seen as being in control of his or her own actions. Further, when I intend to do something, this intention settles, in some sense, what I will do. In Bratman's terms, I have set a plan or course of action for myself. But how, then, can I intend that *we* do something? There is something in this scenario that is out of my control. My intention that we J cannot settle what we will do because you have an equally important role in settling what will be done. Thus, I cannot intend that we J.

Stoutland puts the problem a bit differently by emphasizing that Bratman's attempt to identify a set of individual intentions with common contents is impossible – Bratman (2014) calls this the own-action condition. Because intention makes an implicit reference to the subject that fulfills the intention, there are no intentions with common content. "Art can intend to go to a film and Mary can intend to do the same; but their intentions do not have common content, since Art's intention is *his* going to the film and Mary's is *her* going to the film" (Stoutland, 1997, p. 56).

Bratman has attempted to respond to this line of criticism by pointing out that, when the individual intentions of the form "I intend that we J" are formed, they are done so under the assumption that others in the shared activity will form similar intentions. Bratman stipulates that an agent is typically in a position to predict with some reliability that others have the corresponding intention. Given that all parties form intentions in this way, the shared intention comes into existence, much like Gilbert's joint commitment. Recall, once all members of a group express their willingness to be jointly committed under conditions of common knowledge, a joint commitment comes into being. In this sense participants in a shared intention have a sort of shared control over the matter because each individual intention is dependent upon the others (Bratman, 2007, chap. 8). No one individual controls the others' intention-formation or action. Rather each individual's intentions are understood as partially constitutive of the shared intention.

Still, there is something odd about being able to intend that we J. The issue might become clearer if we think of cases where J is a truly joint action, one that cannot be performed by an individual alone. Consider the act of playing a symphony. Surely playing a symphony is an intentional action. It is not behavior that simply happens to people. Thus, in order to explain this action we must appeal to an intention to play a symphony. But since an individual cannot play a symphony, we cannot reduce the group intention to play a symphony to individual intentions to play a symphony. I cannot, by myself, intend to play a symphony. Further, I cannot intend that we play a symphony. I can only intend to do my part in playing a symphony. But this is not an intention to play a symphony. Thus, the only candidate, according to Bratman's critics (Stoutland, 1997), that is the appropriate subject of the intention is the orchestra. In order to respond to this version of the worry, Bratman has introduced the notion of "intending that." The subject of an "intention that" need not be the person who fulfills the intention. For instance, I can intend that my children clean their room. But it is my children who will fulfill that intention. Shared intentions involve "intending that" rather than "intending to." Stoutland (2008) has argued that this introduces a new attitude altogether, but Bratman's theory requires *intentions to*, not *intentions that*, because only *intentions to* play the necessary role in shaping and informing action.[5]

Like Tuomela's, Bratman's account has been criticized for not being able to handle actions that occur without prior planning (Kutz, 2000). Consider again Searle's group of people in the park. Imagine that instead of being a troupe of actors they are members of the campus safety team. They are meeting together to plan events for the fall semester. During their meeting they notice that a student has accidentally fallen into the lake in the center of the park. Seeing that the student cannot swim and needs help, the members of the safety team spontaneously rush to help the student, coordinating their efforts in such a way as to call 9-1-1, rescue the student, and provide needed care. Is it plausible to think that there was time to form the sorts of shared intentions Bratman identifies? Bratman himself says that his account is a planning theory of shared agency (2014). How, then, does his account accommodate those actions that are unplanned?

The complexity of Bratman's theory, made even more complex in his recent book (2014) by the addition of various notions such as persistence interdependence, also suggests a methodological issue that might need to be addressed. Why start with an analysis of shared intention in pre-planned, complex, adult joint action? Why not start with the phenomenon as it occurs in basic cases and why focus exclusively on the adult case? It may be that there is a core notion of shared intention which helps to explain joint action of various types (planned or unplanned) and by various subjects (adults, children, animals) and upon which one could then build a theory to understand the more complex forms of joint action and shared intention we find in adult human interactions. This doesn't mean that the accounts we have surveyed are wrong. It may be, however, that each provides us with part of a much larger story.

5   Commitment Accounts

In chapter 1 we considered Margaret Gilbert's account of joint commitments. When individuals form joint commitments to do something, believe something, or intend something as a body, they become plural subjects of action, belief, or intention respectively. A joint commitment to intend as a body is a joint commitment made by a collection of individuals to intend some present or future action as a single individual would. Joint commitments are formed when each member expresses his willingness (agrees) to do his part to make it the case that the group intends as a body, in conditions of common knowledge. But such expressions are made conditionally in the sense that each individual makes such an expression of willingness on the understanding that the joint commitment will be in place when and only when each one has made a similar expression. Once everyone has expressed this willingness, a pool of wills is formed and individuals are then jointly committed. Once the joint commitment is established, the individuals are obligated to do their part to make it the case that they intend as a body.

Consider a case in which Joe's construction company intends to build a house for Mrs Wilbur. Each of his employees does not individually intend to build Mrs Wilbur a house. This would lead to the proliferation of Wilbur abodes. Each individually agrees, however, to make it the case that the construction company intends to build it and expresses their willingness to do so on the condition that every other member does the same. Joe's expression of willingness is made simultaneously with every other member's expression of willingness such that these expressions are made under conditions of common knowledge. The members do not need to verbally express their willingness. Often silence is an adequate expression of intention. They must, however, communicate in some way their willingness to be committed with others.

What do individuals actually commit to doing when they commit to doing their part to make it the case that they intend as body? The notion of "doing one's part" remains vague here, and I think suitably so. What one must do in order to "do one's part" in the case of a joint intention to build a house will differ from what one must do in order to "do one's part" in jointly intending to play a game of tennis, for instance. But, just as with group belief, the individuals will be required not to do anything that would undermine the group intention. Consider again Joe's construction company. The company intends to build a house for Mrs Wilbur. If Joe's co-worker Bob fails to show up to begin building or says in public something like "Our construction company won't be building anything for that grump Mrs Wilbur,", then this will undermine the group's joint commitment to intend as a body. He will have fractured the unity of agency formed by the joint commitment. Just as in the case of group belief, the members of Joe's construction company might rebuke him. "Bob!" they might say, "We intend to build this house and build this house we will!"

Critics have charged that Gilbert's account of group intention is redundant. A commitment to do something is basically an intention to do it. David Velleman puts it this way:

For Gilbert, the pooling of wills is the general condition for producing a "plural subject," which can be the subject of shared intention, shared belief, or various other shared states and activities. A shared intention, according to Gilbert, requires not just the pooling of wills but the pooling of wills that are embodied, specifically, in commitments to intend; whereas a shared belief requires the pooling of commitments to believe; and so on. Although I sympathize with Gilbert's desire to explain the sharing of intentional states in general, I think that her interest in generality has led to an account of shared intention that is, in a sense, redundant. Anything that qualifies as a pool of wills, I think, already is a shared intention, without those wills having to be commitments to intend. (1997, p, 30, fn. 4)

Also, Gilbert's account, though it acknowledges groups as legitimate subjects of propositional attitude ascriptions, doesn't really provide us with an account of why group intentions are intentions. This is, perhaps, not something she intended to do. Nevertheless, the following question remains pressing: Are group intentions really intentions?

6   Taking Stock

As we have seen, discussions of group intention are often focused on different things. Since Searle and Bratman deny that groups could be the bearers of mental states, they locate the intentionality of joint action within and among individuals. They provide an account of shared or joint intention rather than of group intention. Tuomela, too, offers an account of joint intention, but he also acknowledges that groups themselves are sometimes the appropriate target of attitude ascriptions, and he offers us an account of group intention that tries to capture the way in which corporate groups (in the sense I have defined) can have intentions. Gilbert also attempts to provide an account of group intention and acknowledges that groups can be the appropriate target of attitude ascription.

It might be useful at this point to introduce another distinction between types of groups. In the introduction to this book

I made a distinction between aggregative groups and corporate groups. Aggregative groups are mere collections of individuals that share a common property – e.g., a collection of all red-haired women. Corporate groups are those that have a structure, an organization (sometimes hierarchical), and a decision-making process, and their identity does not change with a change of membership. They are enduring groups and they exhibit a sustained pattern of behavior. A group that acted only once would not be a corporate group. But the discussions of shared intention, joint intention, and we-intention we have surveyed suggest that the focus there is not on corporate groups but on what we might call plural groups.[6] Plural groups take the third-person plural "they," whereas the corporate agent can be identified as a singular agent, an "it." Plural groups can come into being by mere joint actions. If my husband and I move a table from the downstairs den to an upstairs bedroom we might form, for a time, a plural group, and such a formation might involve the sorts of group ends, shared intention, joint commitments, or we-intentions identified by the theories we canvassed above. Corporate groups are not transitory or ephemeral. They exist despite a change of membership, and one joint action does not bring about a corporate group. Corporate groups require a pattern of behavior that exhibits a unity of agency over time.

The performance of joint actions on the basis of group ends, shared intentions, joint commitments, or we-intentions might very well be the way in which corporate agents form and sustain their agency over time. Plural agents may be the guts of corporate agents. That is, group ends, joint commitments, shared intentional activity, and we-intentions might all be part of what is happening internally within corporate groups, and this produces a pattern of group behavior that exhibits unified agency.

Like the accounts of group belief in chapter 1, the accounts of group intention surveyed in this chapter try to explain what is happening within the group and among the individuals and can help us to understand the ways that group intentions and beliefs are formed. Given the variety of different groups, we might be ecumenical about things and say that group intentions and beliefs could be formed in multiple ways depending on the sorts of subjects and groups involved. But, no matter how compelling the accounts of how groups form their beliefs and intentions, there remains a pressing question: Do groups really have beliefs and intentions?

One approach to answering this question is to ask, first, what function belief and intention play within a subject and, then, whether some arrangement of individual attitudes might play that same role within a group. Velleman (1997) takes this approach:

> I think the conditional commitments described by Gilbert may in fact combine to form such a jointly held representation. Speaking roughly for a moment, I would put it like this. When one agent says "I will if you will" and the other says "Well, I will if you will," their speech acts combine to produce a single story, just as when you start telling an anecdote and your spouse finishes it for you. Speaking roughly, I would say that these two utterances combine to form a verbal representation that's equivalent to the content "We will." If this representation plays the right causal role, by prompting the behavior it represents, and if it also represents itself as playing that role, then it will just *be* an intention – or at least it will be everything that an intention is except mental if anyone still wants to quibble about that term. (1997, pp. 38–9)

As we shall see, philosophers *do* want to quibble about that term. But Velleman's suggestion introduces the functionalist approach to mental states and mind we will discuss in chapter 4. If we define mental states in terms of the role they play in a system rather than what they are made of (brain states, for instance), then this might just open the door to the possibility that groups can be "minded" in the way that individuals are.

7 Suggestions for Further Reading

Recent books by Michael Bratman (2014), Raimo Tuomela (2013), Margaret Gilbert (2013) and John Searle (2010) are the best places to start to dig deeper into the literature. For those who are inclined toward methodological individualism see Miller (1995). For a lovely overview of topics in an area of collective intentionality, including shared agency, see Roth (2010) and Schwiekard and Schmid (2013).

8 Discussion Questions

1 Do we always form an intention prior to performing an action? Can there be actions that are unintentional? Are such things actions or accidents?
2 When you play a competitive game (i.e., chess), are you sharing intentions with your opponent? Explain your answer.
3 What reason is there to move beyond shared intention to group intention?
4 Do you think we are capable of forming beliefs and intentions from the we-mode? Do you have we-intentions?
5 Can you intend to do something that you cannot do? For instance, can you intend to jump 1,000 feet in the air? Can you intend to do something that you cannot do without others?

3
Group Agency

One way to conceive of the accounts we have surveyed so far is to see them as accounts of the various ways in which the beliefs and intentions of a group might be formed and sustained. But are group intentions and group beliefs really beliefs and intentions? And are groups intentional agents, capable of acting on beliefs and intentions in order to bring about change in their environment? Answering these questions depends on what one takes mental states to be and how one defines intentional agency.

1 Some Preliminaries

First, let's consider all the different types of mental states. Here are some examples:

Believing that Boston is the capital of Massachusetts
The experience of seeing the Statue of Liberty
Remembering your first kiss
Intending to cook a pot roast
Wanting to travel to Greece
Pain
Anger
Fear

Many mental states are what philosophers call intentional states. They are about – or represent – things and states of affairs. They take things to be *thus and so*, and they can fail to represent these things correctly. If I believe that Beverly is the capital of Massachusetts I will have a false belief. We discussed this when we examined the nature of belief in chapter 1. Believing, intending, remembering, wanting are all propositional attitudes. They involve taking a stance toward a certain proposition.

Many mental states are also conscious and have a qualitative "feel" to them. Philosophers call this phenomenal consciousness. Consider the experience of seeing the Statue of Liberty. There are distinctive perceptual experiences that feel a certain way. Likewise, pain, anger, and fear all have a qualitative feel to them. The nature of phenomenal consciousness, the what it is likeness of mental life, is the topic of much debate. It is often referred to as the "hard problem" because consciousness is thought to resist any neat reduction to the physical (Chalmers, 1996).

What is the relationship between propositional attitudes and phenomenally conscious states? Debates rage over this question (What question do philosophers not debate?). It seems obvious to many philosophers that conscious states are intentional. The experience of seeing the Statue of Liberty has, at least, in part a representational content – one that represents the Statue of Liberty as thus and so. But do propositional attitudes have a qualitative feel to them? Or, rather, do they necessarily have such a qualitative feel? It seems clear that remembering my first kiss might be accompanied by various qualitative experiences, but it also seems clear that it need not be. I could just remember the event without feeling a thing. Likewise, believing that Boston is the capital of Massachusetts seems to have no particular quality to it. Even when such a belief is something occurrent, something I consciously think about and form at a particular time, it doesn't seem to have a unique qualitative feel to it – not like being in pain. It might feel like something to be a thinker that has the occurrent belief that Boston is the capital of Massachusetts, but the actual belief itself seems to have no qualitative feel to it. Even desire seems like something I could have without a unique qualitative feel to it. I want to visit Greece with my daughter. In thinking about this possibility I might feel a longing, but I need not. Many philosophers find these considerations compelling and will agree that phenomenal consciousness is not essential to propositional attitudes. One could have certain propositional attitudes without feeling a thing. In general, discussions of the nature of mind often deal with these two sorts of states in isolation from each other.

But surely, you might insist, an agent must be *conscious* in order to have beliefs, intentions, and so on? This depends on what one means by conscious. Ned Block (2008) makes a nice distinction between access consciousness and phenomenal consciousness. Access consciousness refers to the way in which states are available for use in a cognitive system. Access consciousness seems required for intentional agency, but phenomenal consciousness (the qualitative feel of states), according to Block and many others, is not necessary for propositional attitudes.

One reason for tackling the issue of propositional attitudes apart from the question of consciousness is that it seems possible that very sophisticated computers and robots have intentional states despite the fact that they are not conscious and do not feel pain or experience the qualitative aspects of seeing. Consider a robot that manages to get around obstacles in its environment. To do so it surely represents the world in various ways and has access to those representations and so has what Ned Block calls access consciousness. These states might be very simple but they meet the criterion for being intentional states; they represent the world and can be true or false. Or consider a more sophisticated case of artificial intelligence – Data, from *Star Trek*. Data is an intelligent agent exhibiting intentionality as well as complex cognitive processing, but he doesn't feel anything. Indeed, his lack of qualitative experience often means he is unable to understand his human counterparts. Now Data isn't real. This is a fictional case. But Data does seem to be a conceptual possibility. It isn't conceptually impossible to imagine a creature that has propositional attitudes but lacks the sorts of qualitative experiences we undergo on a daily basis. If this is so, then it suggests that phenomenal consciousness is not required for agency.

If you are a person who thinks that propositional attitudes are states only of phenomenally conscious beings, then group mental states are going to be a particularly difficult thing for you to swallow. This book isn't going to help it go down any easier. Indeed, I don't intend to argue that groups are phenomenally conscious agents. I don't think a group experiences anything except through its members. But I, like many other philosophers (and cognitive scientists), think that a subject can be an intentional agent without also being a phenomenally conscious agent. My discussion of propositional attitudes will, therefore, assume that they need not be phenomenally conscious states. This might be where some members of the jury stand and leave the courtroom. My approach, however, is not without precedent.[1]

2 French on Group Agency

To ask if groups can have mental states is to ask if they are agents that act for reasons. Agency refers to the capacity to act, to bring about change in one's environment and to respond to stimuli in pursuit of goals on the basis of states such as belief, intention, and desire. What makes such agency intentional is its purposefulness and the fact that it is guided by states that are "about" the world (and ourselves in it). At this level of description the class of agents is quite large. My computer, my dog, a goldfish, an infant, and my husband are all agents. The history of philosophy is strewn with attempts to identify the sufficient and necessary conditions for agency, particularly the sort of agency that is thought to be uniquely human. But agency is best thought of as a spectrum, with very simple agents at one end and very complex agents at the other. Perhaps the very complex ones are conscious and the simple ones are not. Agency isn't an on and off switch. It is rather like one of those dimmers that provides for various levels of ambience. A goldfish is rather dim; my readers, very bright.[2]

One of the most important accounts of group agency can be found in the work of Peter French (1995). French's focus is on the corporation. After establishing that corporations are intentional agents, he goes on to argue that corporations are full-fledged members of the moral community. We will consider his account of corporate moral responsibility in chapter 5. Here I will focus on his account of corporate intentional agency.

French begins by defining the notion of an actor. Actors, according to French, display the following three capacities:

1   Intentionality: to be an actor is to act intentionally – to do something on purpose or for a reason, or with the intention of doing so.
2   Rationality: the ability to make rational decisions and to consider reasons regarding intentions, in particular an actor is able to be responsive to arguments that concern the ways that they can realize their short-term and long-term interests.
3   Actors must be able to respond to criticism. They must be able to adjust their behavior in response to argument. Call this capacity reasons-responsiveness. (French, 1995, pp. 10–12)

He argues that corporations exhibit all of these capacities and hence they are actors. First, corporations have intentions. They have goals and plans that structure the way that they act. The intentions of a corporation are often laid out explicitly in the corporate charter, in strategic planning documents, in corporate advertisements. In addition, French appeals to the notion of intentional redescription in order to show how the actions of individual members of the corporation can be redescribed as the intentional actions of the corporation. Just as the physical actions of an individual human being – the raising of an arm, for instance – can be truly redescribed as an intentional action such as hailing a cab, so the various actions of individual employees, according to French, can be truly redescribed as the intentional action of a corporation. What licenses such a redescription, what makes such a redescription true, is the corporate internal decision structure, or CID. We need not get bogged down in the details of corporate structure here. The point is that French appeals to the fact that events have many different descriptions. Under some descriptions actions are intentional, under others they are not intentional. Princess Leia intended to kiss Luke Skywalker (in episode V) but she did not intend to kiss her brother (even though her brother and Luke Skywalker – unbeknownst to her – were one and the same). To describe her as intentionally kissing her brother would be a false description (and creepy!). According to French, the CID allows for the correct redescription of individual actions as the intentional action of the corporation.

What about the capacity for rational decision-making? Again, the CID structure can be appealed to here. It provides the rules for how decisions are made in a corporation and outlines procedures for considering evidence and reasons that might compromise the interests of the corporation. Likewise the CID allows for the redescription of individual reasons-responsiveness to be the corporation responding to reasons. I recently wrote a letter to my dry cleaners – A+ Dry Cleaners – complaining about the fact that they lost the belt to a beloved wool coat. I received a letter back from Richard Elias, manager of the dry cleaning company with an apology. Alas, no belt. According to French, it is precisely the CID structure, its specification of rules and procedures for responding to complaints and criticisms, that makes it proper to redescribe this as having received an apology from A+ Dry Cleaning. Indeed, this seems the natural way of thinking about the response I received. Poor Richard probably had nothing to do with the loss of my belt. He isn't apologizing to me. He might feel regret that such a thing happened, but he isn't personally apologizing. He is apologizing on behalf of A+ Dry Cleaning. His action of writing the letter constitutes the apology of A+ Dry Cleaning, and it does so because of the rules and policies found in the CID structure.

According to French, then, corporations are intentional agents – actors. I think French is right, and my own views have been heavily influenced by his work. Nonetheless, there are various reasons for wanting to go beyond French here. First, the focus on corporations is a bit limiting. What about other sorts of groups? I suspect French would agree that such groups could be actors as well, but we don't have a sense of what would license the redescription of individual intentions as the intentions of the research group, for instance. Second, what is it, exactly, that licenses the redescription in the case of corporate intentional actions? Not any redescription of an event will result in a true description. We can't redescribe Princess Leia as intentionally kissing her brother, because she didn't know it was her brother. Redescriptions that result in intentional ascriptions seem responsive to things such as beliefs, desires, and knowledge. But, as we have seen, French doesn't take up these issues directly. Indeed, he seems to suggest that, if corporate intentional action requires beliefs and desires, we will be at a loss to talk of corporate actors:

> It should be expected that those who interpret intention on the popular desire belief model would think that talk of corporate intentions (and so corporate actors) must be metaphorical or reducible to the intentions of humans who have the requisite desires and beliefs. Obviously, corporations cannot, in any normal sense, desire and believe. If intentional action must reduce to desires and beliefs, then corporations will fail to make it as intentional actors. But I agree with Bratman that desire-belief theory should be rejected. (French, 1995, p. 11)

I suspect French takes this stance because, like many people, he thinks that beliefs and desires are internal states of the mind. Corporations don't have minds or brains, so how can they have mental states? But how could one be an intentional actor without also being a believer, a knower or cognizer, a thing that forms goals (desires) and pursues those goals on the basis of the beliefs it has? According to some philosophers, belief is basic (Davidson, 1975). In order to intend anything at all I have to be a believer. I can't intend to open a window without also having beliefs about what a window is and how to open it. If groups can be intentional agents, we need a way of understanding how they can have beliefs.

3   List and Pettit on Group Agency

More recently, Christian List and Philip Pettit have argued that certain groups are agents (2011). As French does, List and Pettit begin with a general theory of agency. An agent has four things:

1 representational states such as belief that represent how the world is;
2 motivational states such as desires;
3 the capacity to process representations and act on the basis of them;
4 minimal rationality, attitude to fact, attitude to action, and attitude-to-attitude standards of rationality.

For List and Pettit, the representational and motivational states specified in requirements 1 and 2 are functional states, realized by physical states but not necessarily brain states. "They may be electronic or neural configurations of the agent, for example, depending on its robotic or animal nature. They may be localized in the agent's brain or central processing system or dispersed throughout its body. We require only that they be configurations of the agent – or perhaps configurations of the agent in context – that play the appropriate functional role" (2011, p. 21). We will have more to say about this approach in chapter 4. The third requirement specifies that an agent needs to process its representational and motivational states in a way that leads to action. In humans, such processing is often performed through reasoning or deliberation. In short, agents need to be cognizers. The final requirement requires a minimum of rationality. There must be a coherence and consistency between the beliefs formed (attitude to attitude), between the attitudes and the actions chosen (means–end consistency), and between the attitude and the world (an agent can't be a system that radically misrepresents the environment).

How does such a basic account of agency extend to groups? Unlike French, List and Pettit focus on a broad range of groups. They do, however, limit their discussion to groups that survive a change in membership. Although they note that group agents might be formed by evolutionary pressures or by the design of a mastermind that keeps the members ignorant of their role in the actions of the agent, most group agents are formed via members jointly intending to form a group agent. List and Pettit offer a general account of the conditions for joint intention. Each member, or some suitable subset of the members, agrees to do his or her part to make it the case that they form a unified subject of belief and desire, and each does so with the knowledge that others also have the intention of doing so and are aware of the intentions to do so of others. List and Pettit provide a way to integrate theories of joint intention within a theory of group agency. As I have suggested, joint intentions and joint commitments of the sort we considered in chapters 1 and 2 may best be understood as the mechanism by which individuals fuse themselves into a unity and thereby become intentional agents and the subject of mental state attribution.

Group agents form attitudes (beliefs and desires) via communication among their members, and this communication can take several forms. Deliberation may occur among members, or voting or a dictator may determine the group's judgments. What is important for List and Pettit is that the attitudes, both the beliefs and desires, of a group will often be different (and even in conflict) with the attitudes of individual members, showing that group attitudes cannot be reduced to the attitudes of group members. List and Pettit use the phenomenon of judgment aggregation to make this argument.

Recent work in jurisprudence (Kornhauser and Sager 1986, 1993; Chapman 1998) has identified an interesting paradox that arises when a group of judges arrives at a verdict based on previous judgments regarding the factors that ought to determine the resolution of a case. The judges vote on whether the relevant factors obtain and then let their votes on those issues determine what the verdict should be. This way of determining the verdict can lead to results that differ from those they would arrive at if the judges made individual decisions on the case and then aggregated the votes. Indeed, in many cases there is a stark discontinuity between what each individual judge believes regarding the verdict and what the court decides jointly regarding the verdict. Consider the following example found in Pettit (2003).

A panel of judges must find the defendant liable if and only if it finds, (1) that the defendant was negligent and that her negligence was responsible for the injury to the plaintiff and (2) that the defendant had a duty to care for the plaintiff. Imagine that the judges A, B, and C vote on those issues and on the related matter of whether the defendant is liable.

	Cause of harm?	Duty to care?	Liable for harm?
A	Yes	No	No
B	No	Yes	No
C	Yes	Yes	Yes

There are two ways that the court might make its decision. The judges might vote simply on the issue of liability. They would engage in deliberations about the case and the relevant issues and arrive at their independent judgments in, let us suppose, a perfectly rational manner. Then they would aggregate their votes with respect to the issue of liability and let the majority view on that issue determine the court's decision. Call this the conclusion-driven approach. Given the above matrix and this approach, the defendant would not be found liable, since there are two votes against liability. The court could also aggregate the votes with respect to the individual issues of causation and duty and let the conclusion be accepted – that the defendant is guilty – if and only if a majority endorses both premises. Call this the premise-driven approach. Since each premise does have majority support, the defendant would be found guilty on this approach. If it adopts the conclusion-driven approach, the court will be endorsing a conclusion that is inconsistent with how the majority voted regarding the related issues. If the court adopts the premise-driven approach, then the judges may jointly endorse a conclusion that a majority of them individually reject. This is the paradox. The research on decision-making reveals that the courts often adopt the premise-driven approach. But how could the court rule that the defendant is guilty if no individual judge believes that the evidence supports such a verdict? What could be the justification for adopting the premise-driven approach?

The justification for the premise-driven approach becomes apparent when we acknowledge that the norms of rationality apply to groups as well as to individuals. Just as individual judgments are governed by considerations of consistency and coherency, group judgments are governed by the same constraints. If the court has already established that the relevant issues will determine the verdict, the judges cannot simply disregard the fact that a majority believes that the relevant factors obtain. The premise-driven approach avoids the possibility that the court jointly endorses an inconsistent or incoherent set of propositions. It is an approach that preserves the rationality of the group.

The irrationality of the conclusion-driven approach can be seen more clearly if we consider diachronic rather than synchronic cases. In these cases the verdict is determined on the basis of precedence or previous court judgments, some of which may not be the judgments of the current court. Adopting the conclusion-driven approach will often result in a complete disregard of previous decisions made by a group. The current decision, therefore, will not cohere with past judgments made by the court. The court has the option of disregarding its past judgments or reinterpreting them, but such a practice, if it were implemented all the time, would undermine the integrity and identity of the court. The court will not be able to present itself as a credible promoter of its purpose (whatever that purpose may be) if it tolerates inconsistency or incoherence in its judgments across time. The need to make decisions that cohere with past and present judgments will, therefore, force courts to "collectivize" reason.

The legal paradox is rather perplexing. It turns out that courts can make judgments that are rejected by each of their members. Even more relevant, however, is the fact that the paradox is not restricted to legal contexts. As List and Pettit point out, the paradox will arise in any group that engages in deliberation and decision-making in the context of pursuing some goal or purpose. And, just as the courts are frequently forced to collectivize reason and adopt the premise-driven approach, so too are these groups.

Consider groups that must make a certain decision on the basis of considerations that have been determined by an external authority: admissions committees and promotions committees; committees that must decide the winner of a contest; trusts that have to make judgments on the basis of a trustee's instructions; search committees that must obey standards of hiring set by another department. With all of these groups there is a possibility that there will be a conflict between rationality at the individual and group level. If they adopt the conclusion-driven approach, they run the risk of jointly endorsing inconsistent or incoherent sets of propositions. No group can continually endorse inconsistent or incoherent sets of propositions and continue to pursue its goals. It must, at times, adopt the premise-driven approach and seek consistency in its judgments as a group rather than as individuals.

Consider the following example. A committee of three has been formed to evaluate applications for admission and decide which applicants will be accepted into the philosophy program. The department has previously specified that admission decisions will be made based on the following four criteria: high standardized test scores, grades, letters of recommendation, and a writing sample. If a committee member thinks that a candidate's application is very weak with respect to any of these criteria, then they will vote against the candidate. The committee members (labeled 1, 2, 3) consider each candidate and vote either "yes" or "no" depending on whether the candidate meets the criterion and then on whether they should be accepted into the program. Consider these results for candidate A.

	High test scores?	Good grades?	Good letters?	Writing sample?	Accept?
1	Yes	No	Yes	No	No
2	No	Yes	Yes	Yes	No
3	Yes	Yes	No	Yes	No

In this scenario, each individual thinks that candidate A should not be accepted yet, if we consider how the individuals voted with respect to the criteria, we see that a majority support each of the premises. There are two ways the committee might arrive at a decision concerning candidate A. The decision could be based solely on how the committee members voted with respect to the final question of acceptance, and so the group decision would be "no." But the committee could also let the views of the members on the premises determine the decision regarding acceptance, and then the group decision would be "yes." These two choices correspond to standard group decision-making processes. The latter approach is followed when a committee engages in deliberation and then votes on one issue. The former approach is followed when a committee Chair, for instance, tallies the votes made on independent issues and then lets logic determine what the group decision will be. When we aggregate the premise judgments, however, we get a different conclusion from that derived from aggregating the conclusion judgments. If we determine the group view by appealing to how members vote on the conclusion (conclusion approach), then we ignore the fact that a majority endorses the premises. The group decision would be inconsistent and would not cohere with the premises. If we determine the group decision by appealing to the premises (premise approach), then we arrive at a group decision that no one individually supports.

According to List and Pettit, groups are often forced to adopt the premise approach because they are governed by rationality constraints at the group level. Recall the rationality constraints of attitude to fact, attitude to action, and attitude to attitude, discussed above. List and Pettit provide the following extension to groups:

1 On the attitude to fact front, the group must ensure, as far as possible, that its beliefs are true about the world it inhabits and ideally that its desires are at least in principle realizable. (2011, p. 36)
2 On the attitude to action front, the group must ensure, as far as possible, that whenever its attitudes require an action, suitable members or employees are selected and authorized to take the required action. (Ibid., p. 37)
3 The group must ensure that whatever beliefs and desires that it comes to hold form a coherent whole. (Ibid.)

Consider a department committee that was charged with forming the long-term goals of the department. These goals specified that the next person to be hired was to be in continental philosophy rather than analytic philosophy. The goal was agreed upon by all of the faculty members. Now suppose that, in the course of searching for a candidate, a majority of the faculty votes to hire an analytic philosopher (perhaps their candidate pool was diverse and included such candidates). If the department moves forward with this hire they will have undermined the intention to hire in continental philosophy. Now there may be reasons for doing so (just as there are reasons at the level of an individual to change one's mind), but a group that consistently acts against its desires or goals or that forms beliefs that contradict the beliefs it has previously formed will undermine its own agency. This is the way in which group attitudes are distinct from the attitudes of group members. They are subject to normative constraints that apply to the group.

List and Pettit's approach provides us with a general account of agency from which to consider the case of corporate groups. If we start with a notion of agency that requires, for instance, consciousness, we have ruled out groups from the start. List and Pettit also provide us with an understanding of the role rationality plays in agency and how the normative constraints of coherency, consistency, means–end consistency, and truth can apply to groups rather than just to the individuals within those groups.

List and Pettit are not without their critics, however. There have been various attempts to question the theory of aggregative judgment on which they rest their case (e.g., Cariani 2012), and the focus on formal judgment aggregation has seemed to many to be unnecessarily narrow and to miss something crucial about group agency. Carol Rovane (2014), for instance, has argued that what is needed for group agency is a forging of a unified perspective, and this occurs not through voting but through joint deliberation. It is in the process of agents deliberating among themselves that the unification of several distinct perspectives can come together into a unified perspective. One might also argue that the procedures that give rise to corporate agents, according to List and Pettit, could only plausibly be adopted by something that was already a unified rational agent, and so in terms of giving an account of group agency these authors have failed.[3]

Methodological individualists insist that we can give an account of the premise-driven and conclusion-driven approaches in purely individualistic terms, and there is no need to posit a unified agent that reasons. Miller and Makela (2005) write:

> The second process is to reason individually from a set of premises to a conclusion. Assuming that the conclusion

follows from the premises as a matter of logic, and that the workers are logically competent, then each will individually derive the conclusion from the premises, and do so irrespective of whether the premise-driven or the conclusion-driven way is being used. Of course, in the case of the premise-driven way, the premises from which each worker will individually infer the conclusion are premises determined by voting, whereas in the case of the conclusion-driven way, the conclusion is inferred from premises that have been individually chosen. But the important point is that in both cases the only processes of reasoning going on are processes of individual reasoning in the heads of the individual workers; there is no process of group reasoning. (2005, p. 648)[4]

The appeal to voting mechanisms has seemed to many to be individualistic and to undermine the very approach that List and Pettit are trying to establish. In what sense is the "processing" that goes on really a group process? Genuine group agency seems best located in joint deliberative endeavors where the reasoning and cognition is distributive among members of a group.

We are also left with the same question with which we began: What are group beliefs and intentions? From the discussion of representational and motivational states we know that List and Pettit adopt a functionalist account of mental states. But what does this mean exactly and how could a group realize such states? And if, as List and Pettit insist, agency requires the ability to engage in cognition, to "process its representations," then we need to consider how groups could be cognizers.

4 Taking Stock

There is more to intentional agency than just mental states such as belief and intention. French and, more recently, List and Pettit provide a general account of agency and show how it might extend to certain types of groups. Although each account goes a long way to establishing the plausibility of group agency, both fail to provide an explanation of how groups could be the bearer of mental states and engage in cognitive processes such as memory and reasoning. We don't have a real sense of how groups could be "minded" in a way that would make sense of our practice of attributing mental states and processes to them. We need, therefore, to consider theories of the nature of mental states at the individual level in order to see whether such theories could extend to groups, and we need to consider how cognition, something we normally think of as happening within a head, could occur in a group.

5 Suggestions for Further Reading

In addition to the sources cited in the chapter above, see Huebner (2012), Andric (2014), Smith (2012), and the symposium dedicated to List and Pettit's *Group Agency* in the journal *Episteme* (volume 9(3), 2012), as well as List and Pettit's reply to critics in that same issue. For a critical discussion of Peter French's work, see Kerlin (1997).

6 Questions for Discussion

1 Do you think consciousness is required for intentional agency? Why or why not?
2 List and Pettit provide an argument for thinking that in some cases a group's judgment cannot be reduced to the judgment of its members. What is this argument? Are you convinced by it?
3 Can groups engage in reasoning, remembering, inference, and other cognitive processes?
4 Individual human beings have self-knowledge. Do groups have self-knowledge? Is self-knowledge required for intentional agency?
5 Are sophisticated robots intentional agents?

4
Group Cognition

The accounts of agency that were extended to groups in the previous chapter specify that intentional agents have representational states (such as belief) and motivational states (such as goals and desires), are responsive to norms of rationality, and engage in cognition (reasoning, for instance) that allows them to intervene in the environment to bring about change. List and Pettit have argued that group attitudes should be understood as functional states, but what does this mean? What is a functionalist account of mental states and can it really be extended to groups? And what could it mean for a group to engage in cognitive processing? Cognition is generally thought of as something that happens inside the head. But groups don't have heads. This chapter explores recent attempts to make sense of how groups could be cognitive systems – systems with states such as belief and intention (propositional attitudes or "mental" states) and capacities such as reasoning, memory, decision-making, and perception.

1 Functionalism

The seventeenth-century philosopher René Descartes argued that mental states are states of an immaterial soul. The body, a material substance, interacted with the immaterial soul.

Cartesian dualism, as it came to be known, was a popular theory for a long time. It had a rather fatal flaw, however. It couldn't adequately address the issue of mental causation. How, exactly, could something immaterial cause something material to act? The immaterial soul was said to cause the body to move in various ways. But how is that possible? Causation seems to require extension, and by definition the immaterial soul was not extended, not located in space. It is a bit like asking a ghost to open a door. His "hand" would simply pass through the doorknob. The problem of how an immaterial soul and a material body can causally interact, together with the development of the brain sciences, has motivated the view that the mind ought to be associated, somehow, with the brain and body rather than with some sort of immaterial soul.[1] This has spawned a number of different theories.

Type-identity theories, for instance, argue that types of mental states are identical to types of brain states. For any belief that p (for instance), there is a type of brain state N such that, for any x, x believes that p if and only if x is in N (Armstrong, 1980). So, for instance, my son Finn and I both have beliefs about our cat Sophie. In order for us both to believe that "Sophie's breath smells horrible," we would have to be in the same brain or neural state. What exact neural state would be left up to the neurosciences to figure out. If type-identity is true, then, as French suggests, group mental states would be metaphorical at best. But there are reasons for thinking type-identity theories are problematic.

Type-identity runs into the problem of *multiple realizability*, a term first introduced in the 1960s by Hilary Putnam. Putnam (1967) notes the wide variety of creatures that seem capable of experiencing pain (his focus was on conscious mental states, but the argument works as well for intentional states). Humans, bonobos, polar bears, cuckoo birds, snakes, and even snails, seem like reasonable candidates. But then, for the "type-identity" to be true, there must be some physical-chemical kind both common to this wide variety of pain-bearing species and correlated exactly with each occurrence of the mental kind. For the snail and me both to be in pain, we would have to be in the same kind of physical-chemical state. It just seems implausible that there will be a type of physical-chemical state that is the same across all of these species, given the differences in neuroanatomy and physiology. And what about the possibility of silicon-based androids, artificially intelligent electronic robots, and Martians? These all seem to be possible mental state realizers. But they lack "brain states" that are similar to ours at any level of physical description.[2]

In an attempt to account for multiple realizability, token-identity theories propose that, for any token of a belief that p, there is a token of a brain state N with which the belief token is identical. However, different tokens of the same type of belief that p are identical with brain-state tokens of different types. My dog and I might both have the belief that the cat is in the tree, but different physical types realize our token beliefs. Token identity says that each token mental state is identical to some physical state of the subject's brain, but it doesn't require that the physical state be identical to the physical state in some other subject's brain which shares the same type of belief.

But if each token belief is realized by (possibly) disparate physical-chemical types, then why count those two tokens as tokens of the same type? Think of the problem this way: imagine you have two tokens – two coins from two different countries – but they differ radically in their physical instantiation. We might imagine one is made of plastic and the other is made of metal. One is round and the other is square. If their internal structure and properties differ so radically, why would we call them both instances of a coin?

Functionalism is meant to address this concern. If we found out that the two instances played the same role as a coin (both were recognized as pieces in a monetary exchange system, both could be used in Coke machines, added to other coins they increased the amount of buying power you had, and so on), then we would be justified in calling them both a coin regardless of the fact that their physical make-up differed radically. If we define the nature of "coinness" in terms of functional role, we are able to say something more general about the nature of coins. Likewise, if we define mental states in terms of the role that they play, we can be much more liberal about what creatures can have mental states, and we are able to say what it is about token instances that makes them similar enough to count as the same type of state.

Functionalism is the view that mental states are to be defined in terms of what they do rather than in terms of their physical make-up. For instance, what makes a belief that p the state that it is, is its relation to sensory input, to other inner states, and to behavior (output). The belief that it is raining, for example, might typically be caused by a certain sensory input (drops of water falling from the sky), cause other inner states (such as a desire to stay dry) and result in typical behavioral outputs (reaching for the umbrella). All sorts of different types of physical states might play these causal roles, just as one software program (Adobe Acrobat) can run on various types of hardware (Macs and PCs).

This brief discussion of theories of the nature of mental states puts us in a position now to consider the question of whether groups can have mental states. Token and type-identity theories seem to rule out the possibility of group mental states, as they require that mental state types or mental state tokens be identical with states of the brain. Groups don't have brains. It is difficult, then, to see how they could have mental states according to any version of the identity theory. Functionalism, on the other hand, seems to open up the possibility that groups could have mental states. If functionalism puts no constraints on the "stuff" that realizes functional roles, then it seems as if groups might be the sort of "stuff" that could realize functional roles, and hence mental states. As long as there is some state within the group that is playing the appropriate functional role, it will count as a mental state, regardless of the fact that it is not a state of a brain.

But how are these functional roles to be characterized? Psycho-functionalism is the view that mental states should be defined by their role in a cognitive psychological theory. According to psycho-functionalism, mental states are just those entities, with just those properties, postulated by the best scientific explanation of human behavior. Functional characterizations of mental states should make use of information available from scientific experimentation rather than relying on intuitions about typical causes and typical behavioral effects. Psycho-functionalism will allow us to provide a more fine-grained functional characterization because it will actually identify the typical inputs, outputs, and internal relations between states.

Psycho-functionalism poses a problem for advocates of group mental states, however. Some philosophers have argued that our best scientific explanations of human behavior put mental states within a biological system (Adams and Aizawa, 2008; Rupert, 2009) inside the brain or head of an organism. If this is true, it will be difficult to make sense of how groups can have mental states, since groups don't have brains or heads, or skin and bones. There is a significant and important thesis in cognitive science, however, which suggests that the mind is not bounded by skin and bones.

2   Extending the Mind

Active externalism is the view that aspects of an individual's environment, to which the individual is linked in a two-way interaction, are as much a part of human cognition as are other parts of the human brain. We form *coupled systems* with artifacts, and cognition is distributed across this system. Cognition, therefore, can extend beyond the boundaries of the skin. One of the most compelling defenses of active externalism can be found in the work of Andy Clark and David Chalmers (1998).

Clark and Chalmers argue for active externalism on the basis of several thought experiments. The first involves a video game that was popular during the 1980s. Tetris involves manipulating falling objects in order to make them fit into an arrangement of objects on the bottom of the screen. As the objects begin falling at an increased speed, the task becomes more difficult. There are two options for the manipulation of the objects: one can either (1) mentally rotate the shapes in order to figure out where they might be placed or (2) use the control button that causes the falling objects to rotate in various ways and make the assessment of fit based on what is seen. Clark and Chalmers ask us to entertain the following additional option. Imagine that (3) sometime in the future a rotation device similar to the one on the computer game is implanted in the brain. The device rotates an image of the object on demand and would be just as quick and easy as using the rotation button. We would simply issue some sort of mental command and the rotation would be completed just as if we had manipulated the control button with our hands.

Clark and Chalmers now ask us to consider the differences between these cases. Case 1 is clearly an instance of mental rotation. It appears to be a paradigm case of mental cognition. Intuition suggests that case 2 is non-mental. After all, the rotation does not occur "inside the mind." What about the case involving the prosthetic rotation device? By stipulation the device does exactly what the device in 2 does. The only difference is that it is lodged in the head. Is this really a difference that matters? If we found an alien species that developed a device such as that in 3 via natural selection, we would, it seems, have no difficulty counting it as a case of mental rotation. So, what then prevents us from saying that case 2 is a case of mental rotation? Is the mere fact that the device is outside the head enough to exclude it from the realm of the mental? It seems not. Clark and Chalmers offer the "parity principle" as a criterion: if, as we confront some task, a part of the world functions as a process which, were it to go on in the head, we would have no hesitation in accepting as part of the cognitive process, then that part of the world is (for that time) part of the cognitive process (1998, p. 644). The use of notebooks, palm pilots, calculators, and other artifacts are not simply tools for aiding our cognitive endeavors. In some cases, they are functionally equivalent to mechanisms such as short-term and long-term memory, mental images, mental calculations, and so on. We would have no problem accepting them as part of the cognitive process if they were located in the head, and so, according to the parity principle, these devices ought to be considered part of the cognitive process of a system that includes both human body and environment.

Clark and Chalmers are quick to note that there are, of course, differences. One obvious difference is that cognitive processes are transportable and easily accessible. Our ability mentally to rotate an image and our imagined alien's ability to rotate can be easily accessed and toted around to manipulate various other geometrical shapes and solve various other problems. This isn't the case with the rotation device attached to the Tetris console, which suggests that it isn't geography that distinguishes internal processes as mental but, rather, the properties of portability and accessibility.

Clark and Chalmers agree and, in order to respond to this worry and to show that it is not just cognition but also states such as belief that are extended, offer this second thought experiment. Consider Inga and Otto. Inga hears about the minimalist exhibit at the Museum of Modern Art in New York (MOMA). She recalls that it is on 53rd Street and, based on her memory, begins her journey to the museum. Otto has a mild form of Alzheimer's. He uses a notebook to record phone numbers, addresses, dates, names, and so on. Because his memory is so poor he carries this notebook with him at all times. When he hears about the minimalist exhibit he pulls out his notebook and looks up the address and then sets out to visit MOMA. Now what is the difference between Otto's use of the notebook and Inga's use of her memory? We would have no trouble explaining Inga's behavior by appeal to her desire to attend the exhibit and the belief that the museum is on 53rd Street. Likewise, we should have no trouble explaining Otto's behavior by appealing to the same desire and belief. The only difference is that, in Otto's case, the belief is stored in his notebook rather than his biological memory. But why should mere geography matter?

One might try to distinguish Otto and Inga by saying that all Otto actually believes is that the notebook has the address and that this, in turn, leads him to look into the notebook and form the *new* belief about the actual street address. This story is what Clark (2010) calls the Otto-2 step. He quickly dismisses this move. Note that we can run the same 2-step on Inga. All Inga really believes is that the information is stored in her memory. When she retrieves the information she forms the *new* belief about the street address of the MOMA. But we don't run this story. Indeed, it's a bizarre account of how beliefs in long-term memory explain our behavior. It is highly unlikely that Inga has any beliefs about her long-term memory.

But does this mean that every time we use a computer, rely on a pen and paper to compute a sum, or look up a phone number we form a coupled system? Does my mind extend to encompass the phone book on my phone table? In order to address these worries, Clark and Chalmers (1998) offer the following criteria to be met by non-biological candidates for inclusion into a coupled system:

1   The information must be readily available and be typically relied on. Otto always uses his notebook and carries it with him. He appeals to it on a regular basis when asked questions such as "Do you know ...?"
2   Information that is retrieved must be more or less automatically endorsed. Otto doesn't constantly question whether his notebook is correct.
3   Accessibility. The information must be easily accessed. Otto's notebook is with him at all times and easily accessed.
4   Finally, to avoid some obvious objections involving readily available books and internet search engines, the information contained in the resource must have been previously endorsed by the subject. It is Otto who places the information in his notebook. If it just appeared there we would probably not grant it the same status as that of a belief.

If they are correct that cognition (where that refers to both mental processes and mental states) extends beyond the body, this allows us to understand how groups could have mental states and engage in cognitive processes. Clark and Chalmers focus on the extension of mind to artifacts. But does cognition extend to encompass other people?

Let's begin with the Tetris thought experiment. Recall the three options: (1) mental rotation, (2) rotation by using the control button on the console, (3) rotation by device implanted in the brain. C and C argue that, because we would count (1) and (3) as a case of cognition and the only difference between (2) and (3) is geography, (2) is a form of "mental" rotation. Consider a fourth option: (4) rotation by issuing a command to one's friend who rotates the image for you using the control button on the console. This is not a very efficient way of playing Tetris: options (1), (2), and (3) are clearly faster forms of cognition. But, if (2) counts as cognition, then how can we rule out (4)? If Clark and Chalmers are correct, the mind can extend to encompass other individuals. My Tetris friend and I form a coupled system, and cognition (of a limited sort) is distributed over this system.

One might try to rule (4) out by pointing to the fact that, when another individual enters the scenario, there is a significant difference in control. I can control the button on the computer in a way that I cannot control my friend. My friend can simply refuse to rotate. Computers, assuming they are functioning well, cannot just decide to opt out of the coupled system. But surely our reliance on the functioning of the computer is just as precarious as our reliance on the functioning of a friend. The reason for their malfunction may differ (the computer battery may die, the friend may get annoyed), but in both cases our control of the rotation is somewhat dependent on something outside of us.

But, still, one might argue that my Tetris friend lacks the same sort of portability and accessibility that the Tetris console lacks. I might occasionally play Tetris with my friend, but he is not a "constant" in my life, as required by the criteria Clark and Chalmers established. So let's consider again the case of Otto.

Otto, according to Clark and Chalmers, forms a coupled system with his notebook. Otto's notebook functions in the same way that his long-term memory functions and, according to the parity principle, should be considered part of his mind. Now consider Olaf, who has been married to Inga for thirty years. Olaf doesn't suffer from Alzheimer's disease. He is, however, a philosopher. He often gets lost in his work and has difficulty remembering his appointments, phone numbers, addresses, and so on. But Inga has a sharp mind, and because they spend a great deal of time together Inga provides Olaf with all of the information that he needs in order to get through his day. Indeed, Inga seems to serve exactly the same purpose as Otto's notebook does for him. She is his external memory. Does this mean that Olaf's mind extends into Inga? Do Olaf and Inga form a coupled system? Inga certainly meets the criteria given by Clark and Chalmers.

1   Inga is readily available to Olaf and Olaf typically invokes Inga on a variety of daily details. "Inga, what time is my appointment with the Dean?" "Inga, what is the name of my teaching assistant?"

2   The information that Inga provides Olaf is more or less automatically endorsed. In fact, Olaf has come to rely on Inga so much that he does not even trust his biological memory. He often asks Inga to verify things that he has biologically recalled. "I think I have an appointment Thursday. Is this correct?"

3   Because I have stipulated that Inga is always with Olaf, the information contained in Inga is easy for Olaf to access. Indeed, Inga is much more convenient and reliable than Otto's notebook. After all, Otto needs to retrieve the notebook and then locate where he has put the address. He might forget to bring his notebook or it might go through the wash. This isn't likely to happen with Inga. Because Inga is an active participant in the coupled system of which she is a member, her presence is more reliable than a mere artifact. A loving and committed, cognitive partner, Inga is always there – through sickness, health, and memory loss.

4   Finally, the information that is contained in Inga is information that Olaf previously endorsed at some time or another. Inga isn't making it up as she goes along. Olaf is partly responsible for the storage of this information. "Inga, will you remind me that I have an appointment on Thursday at 4?"

Its seems, then, that, if Clark and Chalmers are correct, the mind can extend not only to encompass non-biological artifacts, forming systems that support cognition and dispositional attitudes such as belief, but also occasionally to encompass other cognitive systems. The argument for the extended mind as developed by Clark and Chalmers rests substantially on the notion of functional equivalence. Otto's notebook forms a coupled system with Otto because it is said to be *functionally equivalent* to his short-term memory. Likewise, Inga and Olaf form a coupled system because the interaction between them is *functionally equivalent* to that found in biological memory (or some part of it). One might argue, however, that coupled systems of either sort (involving just artifacts or involving people) are simply too different to support this claim.

There seem to be two separate issues here. The first is whether the testimony of Inga and the information in Otto's notebook play the same role or have the same function as that contributed by biological memory. The second is whether Inga and the notebook *carry out their function in the same way* that biological memory does. An artificial heart and a biological heart carry out the same function (they pump blood), but arguably they do so in different ways. Now it is true that the coupled systems comprised of Otto and his notebook and Olaf and Inga may differ in the way that they carry out their function (because they have different modules, for instance), but it isn't clear that this means that they are not *functionally equivalent* to a purely biological memory system.

Clark and Chalmers presuppose a common-sense functionalist approach rather than a psycho-functionalist approach. Functional equivalence will be determined by the "causal dynamics" of the case, where the causal dynamics are judged by folk psychological standards. From our perspective as interpreters of behavior, Otto will be guided by the information in his notebook in the same manner as he would be guided by the information in his short-term memory. He will do the same sorts of things, say the same sorts of things, and form the same sorts of propositional attitudes on the basis of the information retrieved from his notebook. This is a loose sense of "causal dynamics," but it is clearly the sense that fuels much of our everyday practice of predicting and explaining people's behavior. I can predict with some accuracy that after Otto looks at his notebook he will head in the direction of the museum. Likewise, in the case of Olaf and Inga, I can predict with great accuracy that Olaf will meet with his assistant on the basis of the information he retrieved from Inga. As Dennett (1987) points out, this practice is extremely successful despite the fact that we know very little about brain processes and "modules." If by "causal dynamics" one means the actual causal mechanisms, and if one requires for functional equivalence that the function be performed by the same mechanism, then accurate judgments of functional equivalency, even among and within uncoupled systems, will be rare indeed.

One might press the worry about functional equivalence by pointing out that the Otto scenario as described by Clark and Chalmers involves a notion of memory that is antiquated.

Biological memory is not a filing cabinet that contains static information waiting to be retrieved. We now know that biological memory is active. It often constructs rather than merely recalls information, and we know that our current goals, moods, beliefs, and so on, influence what is retrieved from memory. But Otto's notebook is passive. It doesn't function in the same way that biological memory does. It doesn't contribute to any reorganization of experience, synthesis with other information, and so on. Thus, Otto's notebook cannot serve the role that biological memory does, and therefore it fails to meet the functional criteria for being part of Otto's mind.

Clark (2010) has responded to this worry in the following way. First, although Otto's notebook is passive, Clark and Chalmers have not claimed that it *is* Otto's long-term memory or that, considered alone, it would be a cognitive system. Rather, Otto's notebook is part of a complex system that involves Otto's brain and nervous system and probably other features of his environment. The notebook plays a role in the cognitive system, and its passivity makes it no less a candidate for playing such a role than the passivity of certain neurons in the brain. I'm rather convinced by this response but note that the objection loses its force when we consider the case of coupled systems involving other people. Unlike Otto's notebook, Inga is active. The addresses, names, numbers, dates, and so on, which Inga contributes are likely to be subject to the same sort of reinterpretations, mergings, and corruptions found in Olaf's biological memory, and this is precisely because the information drawn upon is being stored in Inga's biological memory.

3 From Extended Mind to Group Mind

One might argue, however, that all that has been established is that Olaf's mind extends into Inga's mind. We have extended cognition, but it isn't clear we have group cognition where the cognitive processing is distributed among group members. But imagine that the retrieval and reorganization of information is done by Inga and Olaf jointly – in a dynamic interaction. Olaf can't remember the last name; Inga can't remember the first name. Olaf recalls *where* they met. Inga recalls *why* they met. Through a process of shared deliberation they jointly retrieve, via a process of collective reconstruction, the name of the person. The process of retrieval then is active and not found "inside" the heads of Inga and Olaf. Indeed, it is done via the joint activity of discussion and deliberation that occurs between the two. The interaction is not merely one-way in this case, and the dynamic interaction produces a product not found in either Inga or Olaf. This example takes us from extended cognition with artifacts to extended cognition with other agents. To get to group cognition, we need to have interactive processes among and between group members and cognitive products that arise from these complex interactions.

Our discussion thus far motivates the possibility of mental states extending beyond the boundaries of the skin and motivates the possibility that certain groups could engage in cognitive processes that are distributed across individuals and take place via complex interactions. But is group cognition something that actually occurs in the real world? Daniel Wegner (1987, 1995) and his colleagues (Wegner et al. 1985, 1991) have argued that, through the interactions of individuals' memory systems, larger and more complex memory systems can form. Wegner calls these systems transactive memory systems. His original research is being built on in a variety of different domains, including social and organizational psychology, communications, and management theory (Ren and Argote 2011).

In transactive memory, one individual's memory is shown to function, alongside that of another person or persons, as a kind of socially extended memory system (e.g., Wegner, 1987). Classic examples of transactive memory systems are married couples, who may either have a division of epistemological labor (Wegner, Giuliano, and Hertel, 1985) or rely on each other for dynamic cueing of episodic memories (Hollingshead and Brandon, 2003). These individual memory systems are not merely external storage devices; both the process of remembering and the storage of memories are done in an interactive and dialogical manner. Unlike a notebook, which does not itself have the characteristic of memory identified by mainstream memory research (learning time and access time), a group of individual memory systems can, it seems, become unified and produce a memory product (recall an event, say) that is richer than that recalled by an individual. Consider the case of a department subcommittee charged with revising the department's policies and procedures. Faculty member A might offer some information that he remembers about the history of the department, faculty member B might offer information about what the department Chair requires of the committee, faculty member C might remember something said by the Provost regarding policy-making. As a result the committee might recall a great deal more information relevant to their task than might any one individual, and we can imagine that such recall is done in a collaborative and dialogical process. Information may have been stored in individual minds or heads, but it was retrieved through conversation.

Transactive memory systems as described by Wegner go through the same stages that occur at the individual level: encoding, storage, and retrieval. Encoding at the group level occurs when members discuss information and determine the location and form in which it will be stored within the group. Retrieval involves identification of the location of the information. Retrieval is transactive when the person holding an item internally is not the person who asked to retrieve it. In our case above, a faculty member may have promoted retrieval of information from another faculty member by asking questions and offering alternative hypotheses that the committee member needed to consider.

Individuals in a transactive memory system generally know something about one another's domains of expertise and storage capabilities. Known experts in the group are held responsible for the encoding, storage, and retrieval of domain-specific information. Other members contribute to the storage of information by directing new information to the appropriate expert. When there are no clear experts, other ways of assigning responsibility for the information are used. For example, the person who first introduces the information may, by default, be held responsible for processing that new information. Communication may be crucial to these memory systems, as such systems are formed through a process of interaction over time (Hollingshead and Brandon, 2003). Individuals must, perhaps initially, participate linguistically in transacting collections of information. They must be involved in the allocation of information to specific experts, for instance, and in the determination of what information will be stored.

As Barnier, Sutton, Harris, and Wilson (2008) note, until recently, the results of transactive memory research have been limited, both in methods and in results. The limited results suggest that people in long-term relationships (particularly intimate relationships) perform better on categorized memory tasks than do pairs of strangers (Wegner, Erber, and Raymond, 1991) when the "intimate" pairs are allowed to use their own ways of learning material rather than an imposed structure (Hollingshead, 1998). Such research focuses on the benefits of remembering together and is based on a paradigm that involves individuals jointly memorizing a list of items and comparing the recall on those items with the recall of items memorized alone. More recent research by Sutton, Harris, Keil, and Barnier (2010) suggests that studying people in natural environments yields more significant results. Intimate couples who are allowed to participate in a joint remembering through conversation seem to produce a mnemonic product that is richer than any individual memory (Harris, Keil, Sutton, Barnier, and McIlwain, 2011). In addition, by appealing to research on transactive memory systems in the context of small task groups (Liang, Moreland, and Argote, 1995) Theiner (2013) has argued persuasively for the existence of emergent cognitive properties of these systems. The idea of group cognition, then, is not simply a thought experiment. It appears to be a viable research program.

4 Coarse-Grained Functionalism, Supervenience, and Explanatory Superfluity

Our discussion of the extended mind reveals that the sort of functionalism that allows for beliefs and certain cognitive processes to extend beyond the skin and possibly be realized by groups is a common-sense functionalism, or what we shall call a *coarse-grained functionalism*. According to coarse-grained functionalism (henceforth functionalism), mental states are internal states of an agent that are caused by certain inputs to the system and cause both certain other internal states and certain behavior outputs, where these causal dynamics will be specified by common sense.

If we adopt this way of thinking about mental states and apply it to groups, then group mental states are to be associated with "internal" states of the group that play a certain role. But what is the group "internal stuff" that is realizing the causal roles definitive of mental states? List and Pettit seem to suggest that the formation of group judgments (via the premise-driven approach) somehow realizes group beliefs. Whatever lower-level decision-making processes are happening among and between individuals in a group can be seen as the ways in which the causal/functional roles that define mental states are realized by the group. Indeed, we might view many of the accounts of group belief and intention in chapters 1 and 2 as specifying the way in which groups realize mental states.

Consider, again, Bratman's theory of shared intention. His account says that shared intention is a complex of individual intentional states that are interdependent. This complex plays the same role as intention plays in an individual. The complex of attitudes that Bratman identifies as shared intention, then, can be considered a *realizer* of group intentions. Likewise, Gilbert's joint commitments might be one way in which groups realize certain types of mental states. And we saw that Velleman's attempt to make sense of Gilbert's joint commitments in terms of statements that can represent "we will" relies on the idea that these statements play the same functional role as intention does. We could even see individualistic accounts such as that of Seumas Miller as offering the mechanisms by which group attitudes are realized. Thus, all of these accounts could be consistent with a functionalist approach to group attitudes and cognition. But what is the relationship between these sets of individual, interrelated attitudes (or statements made by attitudes) and group attitudes or mental states?

Functionalists often appeal to the notion of supervenience in order to explain the relationship between the realizers of a mental state and the mental state itself. The basic idea of supervenience is the idea that, if you fix the lower-level properties of some system, you will have fixed the higher-level properties. While the lower-level properties fix the higher-level properties, nothing about the supervenience relation excludes the possibility that the higher-level properties be realized in a number of different lower-level ways. Although functionalists do not want to reduce mental states to brain states, they want to acknowledge that mental states depend on the brain in a significant way. If the brain states change, so will the mental states. List and Pettit use the notion of supervenience to talk about the relationship between the mental states of group members and the mental states of the group. They posit the supervenience thesis (2011 p. 66): "The attitudes and action of a group agent supervene on the contributions of its members."

But there is looming objection here. Jaegwon Kim (1984, 1987, 1988) famously argued that, since it is the realizers of functional states that do the causal work, we ought to identify mental states with their realizers, collapsing functionalism into an identity theory. Applied to the case of group mental states, the objection says that, if what is really doing all the causal work are the attitudes of individuals, then why posit mental states to the group?

List and Pettit deal with this objection by admitting that group mental states (and individual mental states) are not causally efficacious. Instead, they argue that they are causally relevant because they "program" for certain effects. List and Pettit begin by making a distinction between programming cause and implementing cause. Consider a flask that shatters at boiling point. A typical response to the question "Why did the flask break?" is that the water was boiling. But we can get more specific here. The molecules caused the flask to break. The boiling water was certainly causally relevant, but the actual causal mechanism involved molecules. According to List and Pettit, the boiling temperature "programs" for the flask breaking. The molecules implement a program in the same way as software programs my computer to produce a certain image upon my opening it, but the actual implementation of the program involves various electronic signals. The sense in which group mental states are causally relevant, then, is the sense in which the boiling temperature is a cause. Group mental states can program for certain effects even though those effects are ultimately brought about by the mental states of individuals. This proposed solution has seemed unsatisfying to those who want to preserve the causal efficacy of both individual- and group-level mental states.

The real issue here is whether appeal to group-level mental states and cognition plays an explanatory role. If not, they are explanatorily superfluous. A lot rests here on what one takes explanation or "good" explanation to be. If one thinks causal explanation is the only type of explanation, then explanations in terms of group mental states that "program" for effects will seem superfluous. Before we consider some of the objections based on explanatory superfluity and responses to them, it might be useful to look at some explanatory projects that appeal to group cognition.

Edwin Hutchins is a psychologist and cognitive anthropologist at the University of California, San Diego. His *Cognition in the Wild* (1995) is a study of how navigation teams on a US naval vessel use distributed cognition to navigate the ship. His work has been instrumental in developing the field of distributed cognition, which uses various cognitive models, including connectionism and computational models, to understand the complex interactions between group members that bring about group-level behavior (e.g., the steering of a large naval vessel).

A connectionist network is a computational model that involves the synchronous parallel processing among many interrelated simple processing units. The basic idea is that knowledge in very large networks of very simple processing units resides in patterns of connections, not in individuated local symbols. Any unit's activity is dependent upon the activity of neighboring units, connected to it by inhibitory or excitatory links whose strength can vary according to design and/or learning. In a connectionist network, any one unit can represent several different concepts, and the same concept in a different context may activate a slightly different network of units.

Hutchins's early work (1991) used connectionist networks such as the "constraint satisfaction network" to model how groups form interpretations. A constraint satisfaction network is a network in which each unit represents a hypothesis and in which each connection between the units represents constraints among the hypotheses. For instance, if feature B is expected to be present whenever feature A is, there will be a positive connection from the unit that represents the hypothesis that A is present to the unit that represents the hypothesis that B is present. If constraints are weak, then the weights assigned to the connections will be small. If the constraints are strong, the weights assigned to the connections will be large. Inputs can also be thought of as constraints. A positive input means that there is a relevant feature present in the environment. A negative input means the relevant feature is missing. Each unit will adjust its activation on the basis of the activation of the units connected to it and the strengths of the connections to those units and inputs from the environment. The network will then eventually settle into a state in which as many constraints as possible are met. A constraint satisfaction network models, among other things, the way in which a person might arrive at an interpretation or judgment.

Hutchins's work reveals how the constraint satisfaction network model can be used to understand the way that groups arrive at interpretations or judgments. A group-level constraint satisfaction network will involve many sub-networks. These sub-networks represent individuals in the group. The individuals are then connected in various ways, and the connections are given weight depending on whether the connection is one that inhibits or excites. The connections between individual networks represent communication between individuals in the group. There are several communication parameters, including the pattern of interconnections among networks (who talks with whom), the pattern of interconnectivity among the units of communicating nets (what they talk about), the strengths of connections between the nets that communicate (how persuasive they are), and the time course of communication (when they communicate). Altering these patterns has significant consequences for how quickly and efficiently groups arrive at interpretations.

In "The social organization of distributed cognition" (1991) Hutchins argues that confirmation bias, the propensity to affirm prior interpretations and to discount, ignore, and reinterpret counter-evidence to an already formed inter-pretation, occurs at the level of groups. But, by manipulating the communication parameters, his connectionist network models have shown that confirmation bias can be mitigated. For instance, when individual networks have overlapping rather than mutually exclusive task knowledge, they have less of a tendency to ignore counter-evidence. When individuals are aware of one another's expertise and their responsibilities within the group, there is less of a tendency to stick to an inter-pretation and more discussion of alternative interpretations.

So here we have a particular phenomenon, the confirma-tion bias of a group, which is modeled using a connectionist network applied to the group as a whole. Not only do we get an explanation of why confirmation bias occurs in a group, we also get a way to ameliorate that bias by changing the various network connections between individuals. This is the type of explanatory work that is being done in the field of distributed cognition. The question is whether there is any need to appeal to group-level cognition in order to do the explanatory work.

In a series of papers and monographs, Rob Wilson (2001, 2004, 2005) has argued that appeals to group cognition are explanatorily superfluous because we can always show that all that is going on are individual psychological processes within a particular social organization. Wilson argues that appeals to a group or group mind are often confused attempts to state a version of what he calls the *social manifestation thesis*. The social manifestation thesis refers to the claim that individuals have properties that are manifest only when those individuals form part of a group of a certain type. Wilson contrasts this thesis with the group mind thesis, which is the claim that groups have properties, including mental states, that are not reducible to the individual states of individuals. He dismisses the work of Hutchins as evidence of genuine group-level mental phenomena by saying that "the statement 'the crew saw the oncoming ship and decided to change direc-tion' might be made true simply by individual-level psycho-logical facts, together with other, non-psychological facts about social organization" (2004, p. 291).

No doubt some social phenomena can be explained in this way. Whether all of what Hutchins does in *Cognition in the*

Wild can be replaced with such explanations is another issue. Hutchins goes way beyond the simple positing of mental states. His explanation involves appeal to various cognitive models that apply to groups as systematic wholes. Further, the application of cognitive models of decision-making to the group itself seems to yield insightful explanations of group phenomena. Whether there is an equally insightful analysis that involves not viewing the group itself as a constraint satisfaction network remains to be seen. The explanatory adequacy of the empirical work being done on distributed cognition is itself an empirical question. It can't be dismissed wholesale without careful treatment of each explanatory project. The growth of research on distributed cognition seems a clear indication that many people find it explanatorily powerful.

Clearly, though, there are cases of group behavior that can be explained by appeal to individual attitudes and aggregative models (which involve appeal to the social organization of individuals). Huebner (2014) provides an example to motivate this. Consider the operations of a stock market. The market is composed of individual buyers and sellers who are making independent decisions regarding the stocks and bonds that are of interest to them. In the *Wisdom of Crowds*, James Surowiecki (2004) argues that the stock market itself is able to make judgments. When the Challenger space shuttle blew up, the floor of the American stock market went wild. Traders quickly sold shares in four of the corporations associated with building and launching the shuttle. Although the stock of three of those companies stabilized throughout the day, that of the fourth, Morton Thiokol, continued to drop dramatically. According to Surowiecki (2004), the stock market judged that Morton Thiokol was responsible for the disaster. Huebner (2014) argues that this case can be explained merely by aggregating the attitudes of individual agents. There is no need to posit judgments to the stock market, for the judgments of individuals explain it all. But are all social phenomena explainable in terms of individual attitudes and their interaction?

The methodological individualist will answer this question in the affirmative. According to methodological individualism, the actions of groups can be explained by appeal to the judgments, actions, and attitudes of individuals and, on more advanced versions of the theory, the interrelations between them. If we want an explanation of why, for instance, Chrysler merged with Daimler, we ought to find out what the relevant decision-makers believed and their reasons for merging the two companies. Macro-level explanations, according to the methodological individualist, are in principle reducible to micro-level explanations.

Let me offer a reason for thinking that we should be more ecumenical concerning the methodology of the social sciences. Recall the familiar distinction between types and tokens. "Tokens" are particular instances – for example, a particular mental state in an individual or a particular social event such as the 2001 Super Bowl. "Types" are characteristics that tokens share. Thus, the 2001 Super Bowl is an instance of a variety of "types": a Super Bowl game, a football game, and a national pastime. "Types" are general categories under which "token" events can be subsumed. Now it seems quite possible that each token social event can be explained by appeal to the activities and intentional states of individuals. In the same way, it seems possible that token mental states are identical with certain token physical states. The methodological individualist, however, is committed to the micro-reducibility of both token social events and social event types. But it is the reduction of social types that is problematic.

Consider the problem, discussed above, for type-reduction in the philosophy of mind. For any type of mental state – for instance, the belief that grass is green – there are, in principle, many different ways in which this state could be realized. Mental states are multiply realizable. The relationship between mental states and physical states has been described as one of supervenience. Mental states supervene on physical states. If this is so, type-reduction is not possible. There is no reason to believe that the heterogeneous physical states will share enough in common such that there is a specific type of physical state that can be identified with a particular type of mental state.

Social phenomena are also multiply realizable. War, for instance, is clearly a multiply realized phenomenon. How are we to explain war in the twentieth century in its various manifestations without appeal to group-level properties such as the beliefs, policies, and positions of nation-states? If we gave an exhaustive list of the individual intentional states of nation-state members and their various interactions, it would perhaps provide us with a "good" explanation. I can't really conceive of how this would work, but perhaps it is possible to provide such an explanation. The fact is, we don't. We engage in historical and political analysis without seeking out the micro-level realizers of these phenomena. If we are to adopt the criterion of explanation that the critics of group cognition suggest, then we would have to question the methodology of a variety of social sciences, including history, political science, organizational theory, and sociology.

Consider again the merger between Chrysler and Daimler. If a social scientist were interested in explaining that token event, he or she might look to the individual intentional states of decision-makers. But social scientists are not only interested in explaining token social events. They are also concerned with explaining social event types. They are interested in such questions as "Why do firms or companies, in general, merge under certain economic situations and why do nations adopt certain political policies as a result of economic instability?" To answer these questions we cannot appeal to individual intentional states because, in many cases, there may be nothing in common at the micro-level that would explain why these companies or nations acted in the same way. Given the explanatory aims of social sciences, I think there are strong methodological reasons to accept the adequacy of macro-level explanations that appeal to the mental states and processes of groups.

What seems to be fueling skepticism about the explanatory power of appeals to group cognition and mental states is an underlying commitment to a very stringent notion of causal explanation. Good explanations are *causal* explanations, and causal explanations are always found at the level of individual psychology.

In "Beliefs and desires incorporated" (1994) Austen Clark develops this line of argument. According to Clark, the official policy statements of an organization are essential to our practice of predicting its behavior, but such official statements should not be seen as legitimate explanations of the actions of organizations.

It does not seem an adequate explanation of the eventual episodes of gunfire to say that the U.S. government wanted to achieve certain ends. We do not think of the desire as a state of the government, interacting causally with other states, producing the official action ... How do we go about [providing an explanation]? We leave aside the vocabulary of official statements and descend to the level of interactions among people making up the government. (Clark, 1994, p. 419)

If belief/desire explanation is causal explanation, then it doesn't seem right, according to Clark, to explain the actions of organizations in terms of desires and beliefs. How could these group beliefs and desires be causally efficacious in the production of organizational acts? They do not seem to be physical states of the organization, and only physical states (or events) can engage in causal relations. Organizational beliefs and desires are epiphenomenal and hence causally inert according to this objection.[3]

There is an analog of this objection that applies at the level of individual psychology. If one thinks that beliefs and desires are not reducible to brain states (because, for instance, their content is determined by their relation to the environment), then beliefs and desires appear to be epiphenomenal and are not causally responsible for the production of other states and behavior. The need to salvage the causal explanatoriness of belief and desire has led many down a reductionist path. Beliefs and desires, according to reductionism, must be brain states in order for belief/desire explanation to be true causal explanation.[4]

While not decisive, the following line of response suggests that the objection and its analog are less threatening than they first appear. Reductionism is motivated by a view of causality that is too stringent. This point has been made forcefully by Lynne Baker in *Explaining Attitudes* (1995). Baker points out that the conception of causal explanation on which reductionism is based is too restrictive in the sense that it rules out certain types of explanations as causally explanatory. This is *prima facie* unacceptable because these explanations comprise a large collection of successful everyday explanations as well as explanations in economics, politics, and psychology. Such explanations make no reference to intentional states but, nonetheless, presuppose intentional states. Baker uses the following as an example: "Al's application for a gun permit was turned down. The causal explanation is that Al is a convicted felon. If he had not been a convicted felon, he would have received the gun permit" (1995, p. 154). Baker argues that, if we adopt the criterion of causal explanatoriness present in the views of, for instance, Jaegwon Kim (1988), this perfectly good causal explanation must be rejected. This suggests that one ought to reject the accounts of causality underlying the reductionist project. If we adopt a less stringent notion of causality, we can salvage the causal explanatoriness of beliefs and desires at the level of individuals and groups.

5   Group Cognition and Architecture

Still, skepticism remains. In *Cognitive Systems and the Extended Mind* (2009), and in more recent articles (e.g., Rupert, 2011), Robert Rupert defines a cognitive state in terms of its role in a larger system. A state is cognitive, according to Rupert, if and only if "it is the state of one or more of an integrated set of mechanisms that contribute distinctively (i.e. not as background conditions) to the production of a wide range of cognitive phenomena, across a variety of conditions, working together in overlapping subsets" (2011, p. 637). In short, a state is cognitive if it functions within a cognitive system, where the latter involves various mechanisms and processes that "contribute causally to the production of a wide range of cognitive phenomena, across a variety of conditions, working together in an overlapping way with a variety of other mechanisms of similar standing" (Rupert, 2009, 41). Cognitive systems are persistent and display a set of capacities that persist across different contexts. This persistence is best explained, according to Rupert, by the fact that they are realized in a physically bounded organism. This systems-based approach is then used by Rupert to rule out (or at least cast serious doubt on) artifacts such as a cellphone, or a calculator, as part of the cognitive system and activities involving these artifacts as cognitive processes, because such things are not integrated in the ways that, say, vision, linguistic processes, and short-term memory are typically integrated. It is also used to rule out the possibility of group cognitive states and group cognitive systems. Rupert's point here is that it isn't enough to show that groups can realize mental states; we need to show that they are cognitive systems.

Bryce Huebner agrees, and in *Macrocognition* (2014) he tries to show how groups could be cognitive systems. He offers us a sophisticated version of homuncular functionalism – the view that individual minds are "corporate entities" made up of simpler agents carrying out limited computations who contribute to a larger system.[5] According to Huebner, cognitive systems should be understood as parallel processing networks that are composed of numerous discrete subsystems and mechanisms that work relatively independently of one another in order to produce domain-specific representations that result in system-level behavior. Cognitive systems have a "kludgy" architecture. Their components are modules put together haphazardly by evolution. The modules process a narrow range of information, and their outputs are integrated in ways that help an organism cope with change in the environment. For Huebner, even goal-directed behavior is implemented by "massively distributed, highly integrated, specialized, and unconscious computational systems" (2014, p. 79).

Psychological explanation, according to Huebner, is a species of reverse engineering and essentially involves identification of basic cognitive tasks intentionally and functionally specified (solving a math problem, making a cup of espresso – Huebner's favorite example) and explaining these in terms of components that involve subtasks and various computational mechanisms. These in turn will be explained in terms of further functionally specified subtasks to be explained by simpler computational mechanisms until the explanatory project bottoms out "in homunculi so stupid that they can be implemented by on/off switches (or their equivalents)" (Huebner, 2014, p. 65).

According to Huebner, genuine group mentality arises only when groups implement a computationally analogous kind of cognitive architecture to the one found at the level of individual minds and engage in flexible, goal-directed behavior. He turns homuncular functionalism on its head and argues that the "organizational structure" of the individual mind can be writ large within groups. Huebner requires that the following three criteria be met by any putative case of group cognition.

1   There is a computational architecture in the collectivity that consists of a variety of computational subroutines, each of which is dedicated to solving a particular computational task.
2   Each of these subroutines, which are implemented by individuals – or perhaps groups of individuals – and the technological apparatuses that they employ in solving particular sorts of tasks are organized so that their representations are integrated into larger computational structures by way of local interfaces between these subsystems.
3   Each of these interfaces is implemented by a "trading-language" that facilitates the construction of complex representations from local information processing that is (largely) encapsulated and carried on without recourse to the computations responsible for producing representations in other component systems. (2014, p. 84)

Crime scene investigation teams, for instance, appear to implement an architecture that is widely distributed and involves the compartmentalization of individuals with specific tasks and specializations that produce representations, which are then used to produce more complex representations in the form of narratives. Research in high energy physics is undertaken by large research groups, and Huebner tentatively suggests that these groups might approach maximal minds. The distribution of cognitive labor in such groups results in representations that are transferred through various media to form group representations which function to adjust the system's behavior (ibid., p. 254). Further, these groups seem capable in some cases of misrepresenting the world and have various ways of preventing misrepresentation. They seem to respond to the norms of experimentation established within their community and so appear to be reasons responsive.

Though he defends the possibility of group cognitive systems, Huebner thinks these criteria will seldom be met. But mindness, according to Huebner, comes in degrees. Certain cognitive systems will be minimal minds because they do not have robust representational states such as belief, desires, and intentions. Rather they form what Ruth Millikan (1995) calls "pushmi-pullyu" representations. These representations are not decoupled from the immediate features of the environment and lack linguistic structure. Huebner points to the honeybee hive as an example of a minimal mind. According to Huebner, the groups we find in our world may be more like hives than a human mind.

Huebner's skepticism is fueled in part because he adopts a very standard view of cognition that involves the processing of internal representations that carry content. He follows Carruthers (2006, p. 68) and others in thinking that cognition (or at least maximal mindedness) requires that subjects have "distinct belief states and desire states that are discrete, structured, and causally efficacious in virtue of their structural properties." They must be "real" entities that have a structure such that they can represent the world. As Huebner puts it, "on this view, we would need to find discrete *internal* states of a collectivity with the relevant functions that we suppose are necessary for being beliefs and desires of the group" (2014, p. 143; emphasis added). Huebner thinks this is too tall an order. If he is right, we might just have to give up on the idea of genuine group mental states.

6 Taking Stock

We have seen that a coarse-grained functionalism seems, at this point, the only plausible way to make sense of group mental states and cognition. In addition, it needs to be a functionalism that allows for the fact that mental states might be realized by processes outside of the brain. That is, whatever functionalism we adopt has to be amenable to active externalism. Standard functionalism defines mental states in terms of their role in a larger cognitive system. Cognitive systems not only form but also process representations, and we have seen how Huebner and others have tried to show that groups can meet the requirements for such cognitive systems. The arguments made are tentative and conditional. They are conditional because they rest on the truth of coarse-grained functionalism and active externalism, and they are tentative, at least in Huebner's case, because he is skeptical that the sort of structure needed to produce representations that are genuine group mental states can be found in the world.

Where does this leave us? Recall that we started this exploration by considering our practice of ascribing belief and other mental states to certain types of groups. This practice occurs not only in legal contexts, where, say, corporate liability is of concern, but in common-sense explanations of social events we find in the newspaper and in social scientific research. Is this practice justified? If we follow Huebner, it looks as though we will have to say that in many, many cases our attributions are simply false, because the groups in question won't have the requisite architecture to give rise to mental states such as belief.[6]

Further, even if we are more optimistic than Huebner and allow for the attribution of mental states and cognition to a wide variety of groups, this functionalist approach doesn't really seem to fit with our practice of making sense of others in terms of beliefs, intentions, and desires. The point is analogous to one made by Daniel Dennett concerning our practice of ascribing intentional states to individuals. Dennett writes: "we all use folk psychology knowing next to nothing about what actually happens inside people's skulls ... our capacity to use folk psychology is quite unaffected by ignorance about brain processes – or even by large-scale misinformation about brain processes" (Dennett, 1987, p. 48). We are able to explain and predict the behavior of agents extremely well without any knowledge of their brain states or what functional state their brain may be realizing. Our practice seems to move along just fine, and has done so for thousands of years, without any knowledge of what goes on inside the head. Now one way to go is to say that our practice is suboptimal and should be replaced with a science of the mind. This is the view advocated by some eliminativists, who argue that folk psychology – our everyday practice of making sense of others – should be eliminated and replaced with more scientific terms. Eliminativism was all the rage at one point but has lost steam. Most philosophers agree that folk psychology is here to stay. How then do we make sense of others without knowing anything about their internal states? If mental states are brain states or realized by brain states, then it looks as if the concepts we are using to make sense of others are somehow different concepts than those appearing in these theories.

Similarly, our attributions of mental states to groups are made with only a vague idea of the inner workings of the group and often without any information about the actual intentional states of the members. We simply don't have access in many cases to joint commitments and individual decisions to accept a proposition. Yet our explanations of the actions of groups in terms of its beliefs seem to be explanatorily powerful. If we conceive of group mental states as internal states of the group, it is difficult to see how our practice of attributing mental states could reflect these internal states, which remain mostly unknown to us.

The approaches to establishing group mental states and processes have assumed that the only way to justify our practice of making sense of groups is to show that groups meet the criteria for intentional agency, and, as we have seen, these criteria involve the notions of mental representation, cognition, and rationality. But such notions are interpreted in a particular way. These accounts presuppose a hard-core realist view of the mind in which our practice of making sense of others (groups) is justified because there really are states inside the head (or inside the group) that are tracked by our practice. If I predict that you will get an umbrella because I was told you believe it to be raining out, my prediction works, because you have an inner state that *means* it is raining out that causes further mental states – the desire to stay dry, for instance – and causes your actions. If we attribute to Israel the belief that Syria has used chemical weapons, such an ascription is true and has explanatory power only because there is a state internal to the group that *means* Syria has used chemical weapons. Propositional attitudes are seen as internal entities that play a causal role in the production of behavior and whose content is derived through causal relations. This approach to propositional attitudes is what Haugeland (1990) calls neo-Cartesian.

If this is how we are conceiving of beliefs and desires, then, the possibility of group beliefs and intentions seems remote. Indeed, I find it difficult to salvage the explanatory power of individual mental states on this understanding. There is, however, another way of understanding mental states and another way to approach the issue of intentional agency that is worth considering and makes sense of our practice of attributing mental states to individuals and groups. I turn to this approach in the next chapter.

7 Suggestions for Further Reading

For those interested in reading more about the extended mind hypothesis, see Menary (2010), and for an extended defense of the extended mind hypothesis, see Theiner (2011). For those interested in reading more about distributed cognition, Hutchins's *Cognition in the Wild* (1995) is the place to start. Work by Theiner, Allen, and Goldstone (2010) is also essential reading.

8 Questions for Discussion

1 Is functionalism a plausible theory of mental states?
2 Does the mind extend beyond skin and bones? If so, is there a difference between extending my mind to encompass an artifact such as my iPhone and extending my mind to encompass the mind of other human beings?
3 Are appeals to group attitudes explanatorily powerful? Are explanations or theories that apply individual cognitive models to groups explanatorily powerful?
4 Borg is a name for a fictional alien race that is a recurring antagonist in *Star Trek*. It is a collection of individuals that function as drones in the collective or hive. Is the Borg a group mind?
5 What is Rupert's definition of a cognitive system? Why does he think that cognitive systemhood is required for mental states?

5
Interpreting Groups

The approaches to group cognition and group agency we surveyed in chapters 3 and 4 begin with a theory of cognition and agency and attempt to show how groups can meet the criteria laid out in those theories. There is another way to approach the issue of intentional agency, however, and one that I think makes the issue of the intentional agency of groups more tractable. This approach begins with our practice of making sense of others rather than a metaphysical theory of agency or mind. By reflecting on our practice and what has to be the case in order for it to be successful, the nature of intentional agency and mental states is revealed. The approach is called interpretivism.

1 Interpretivism

Interpretivism is the view that, if we can successfully make sense of another being – understand and interpret its behavior by using our folk psychology – it is an *intentional* agent. This view has been developed and defended most notably by Donald Davidson (1973, 1975, 1978), John Haugeland (1990), Daniel Dennett (1987, 1991, 2011) and, more recently, Bruno Mölder (2010). It is an approach to intentionality that starts not with metaphysical speculations about the nature of the mental, but with our practice of attributing intentional states. It asks: What are the constitutive features of our practice that account for its explanatory power? That is, what assumptions do we need to make about an agent in order to interpret her behavior successfully? If interpretation is successful, then the assumptions we make about an agent in the process of interpreting her are justified.

Our practice of making sense of others involves taking what Daniel Dennett (1987) has called the *intentional stance.* When we adopt the intentional stance toward an entity, we attempt to explain and predict its behavior by treating it as if it were a rational agent whose actions are governed by its beliefs, intentions, and desires. Dennett contrasts the intentional stance with two other strategies, the physical stance and the design stance. One day this winter I woke to find that my thermostat was not working. I could have taken the intentional stance toward my thermostat and attributed various beliefs and desires to it. "It doesn't want to turn on because it believes it has been overworked." But these attributions don't really help to explain the behavior of this simple system. In order to understand why it won't work, it would be much more powerful either to take the design stance and consider the design of the thermostat and the various ways in which it is failing to function as it was designed or, like the workman who arrived at my house shortly afterward, to take the physical stance and simply open up the darn thermostat and see what is going on inside it such that it failed to work that morning.

When we attribute intentional states to agents, we do so in order to explain and predict not simply an action or an utterance, but the agent. The subject of intentional state attribution is, then, the whole system or person. When I attribute beliefs and desires to my son, I am attributing them to him, not to his brain or some complex of his brain and nervous system. I want to know why *he* behaved in the manner he did. Reflection on our practice strongly suggests that mental states are not internal states of the brain (either physical or functional) but states of an agent or a system. Whether or not someone believes that p or intends that p does not consist in whether or not a person's brain is in a particular state or realizing a particular functional role.

It consists in what a whole agent will or will not do in situations in which they find themselves.

Reflection, then, suggests that the propositional attitudes on our practice are dispositional states. Dispositional states are functional states of a sort. They characterize how something will behave, or function, under certain circumstances. Consider solubility. Solubility is a property of a substance that is defined in terms of its ability to dissolve under certain types of conditions, namely, when the substance is placed in water. According to this understanding of mental states, to believe that p, for instance, is to be disposed to behave in a certain way and to be in certain other mental states. To believe that "snow is white" is to be disposed to assent to the proposition "snow is white," and to believe that snow is not black, and so on. The dispositions make reference to other mental states since the mental is holistically characterized. Understanding mental states as dispositional states, then, is not simply behaviorism. The difference between functionalism and dispositionalism is that the dispositionalist views mental states as states of whole systems rather than as internal states of the system, and the focus is on the forward-looking causal relations – what a system is disposed to do under certain conditions.

When we adopt the intentional stance toward an agent we posit propositional attitudes, reasons for their behavior. Not just any reasons will do. The reasons must justify the behavior. As Dennett points out, "explanation of actions citing beliefs and desires normally not only describes the provenance of these actions, but at the same time defends them as reasonable under the circumstances" (Dennett, 1987, p. 48). We are not looking simply for reasons why someone would behave in that way (any number of reasons may justify the behavior) but for the reasons *for which* she acted the way that she did. Again, we are interested in *her* reasons not simply reasons *per se*. This, in turn, requires that, when we attribute beliefs, intentions, and desires to an agent in order to provide them with reasons for their behavior, these must be ones that can be seen as intelligible from the agent's perspective as well as our own. We want it to make sense to us that she acted as she did for the reasons she did. Reflection on these cases suggests that an action (including an utterance) will be intelligible to us – in the relevant sense – only if it makes sense *to us* that it made sense *to the agent* that she did what she did. This reflexive constraint guides us in our interpretative endeavors.

In order to make sense of others and hence make their behavior (both linguistic and non-linguistic) intelligible to us in the appropriate way, we must assume that the agent shares our norms of rationality – i.e., that the agent is rational. If we did not make this assumption, the agent's behavior would remain unintelligible to us and interpretation would be undermined. We can only understand the thoughts and words of another if we suppose that their beliefs are incorporated in a pattern that is similar to the pattern of our own beliefs, which is to say, a pattern governed essentially by the norms of consistency and truth.[1] Therefore, the constraints we recognize as applying to our own beliefs, constraints that we could loosely call epistemological, are to be used as constraints on possible interpretations: do not act contrary to your best judgment; draw inductive inferences on the basis of all available, relevant evidence; believe only things you take to be true; don't believe inconsistencies; and so on.

If our explanation of the agent in terms of beliefs and desires makes her behavior intelligible to us only if it can be seen by us as intelligible from the agent's perspective, then our practice of interpretation involves the positing of an alternative point of view – a point of view from which the intelligibility of one's own behavior can be assessed. I am introducing here what many have called a *first-person* point of view. For Locke, a first-person point of view was a phenomenological point of view – a unified consciousness. Contrary to Locke, we need not associate this point of view with consciousness. Nor need we associate it with a soul or brain. A rational point of view is not a point located somewhere inside someone's head or soul. It is a perspective and one that can be adopted by other agents. When we make sense of others, we often project ourselves into their rational point of view in order to be able to better provide reasons that are intelligible in the way the reflexive constraint requires.

A rational point of view, then, is a conceptual point rather than a metaphysical point.[2] It is a perspective from which one can assess one's own cognitive life. If we do not assume that the agent has such a perspective, the rationality constraint and the associated reflexive constraint would have no force. Agents could not be assumed to be governed by our norms of rationality if we did not also assume that they had a rational point of view from which they can assess their beliefs and intentions for consistency, truth, and intelligibility.[3]

Once the assumption of rationality (with its associated assumption of a rational point of view) is in place, we attribute to the agent intentional states that a rational agent *ought* to have. We begin by attributing what beliefs the agent *ought* to have given its environment and function in the world. Then we figure out what desires it *ought* to have given the same considerations. These attributions are made not in isolation but holistically. The assumption of rationality involves the assumption that the agent shares with us a dense pattern of belief and thought, and the contents of thought are, in our everyday practice, attributed on the basis of these other beliefs and their content. Once we have attributed to the agent the beliefs and desires a rational agent *ought* to have, we can predict what a rational agent with those beliefs and desires ought to do or appeal to these beliefs and intentions in order to explain the agent's behavior.

How does one determine what desires and beliefs an agent ought to have? Following Dennett, we can adopt the following guidelines: attribute as beliefs all of the truths relevant to the system's interests that the system's experience to date has revealed. An implication of the intentional stance is that believers believe mostly truths. If we are to attribute the beliefs that a system *ought* to have, then we will not attribute to the system lots of false beliefs. In general, false beliefs will not promote a system's interests and so they are not beliefs a system *ought to have*. This is not to say that we cannot attribute false beliefs but that such attributions are made against the backdrop of mostly true beliefs. If attribution of falsehoods is required, there must be a story to tell that justifies such an attribution. Attribution of desires involves attribution of the most basic desires: survival, absence of pain, procreation, play, etc. And the attribution of absurd or harmful desires requires a special story just as the attribution of false beliefs requires a special story.

The fact that our practice of interpreting others is so successful is evidence that our assumption of rationality is justified. Our interpretative practice works because agents are rational to some extent and designed by evolution to be so. If this is the case, then we need not look for deeper metaphysical facts. The nature of intentionality is revealed in our practice of making sense of others. If the assumption of rationality is justified, then we are dealing with an agent who has a pattern of belief and thought that is similar to our own and that is governed by the same norms of intelligibility. If our best efforts to make sense of an individual fail, then there is no reason to believe that we are dealing with a rational agent and hence there is no reason to believe we are dealing with an intentional agent.

But won't this mean that the class of intentional systems is quite large? After all, we can, it seems, explain the behavior of all sorts of things by adopting this "intentional stance," some of whom we intuitively don't want to admit are intentional agents. We can, for instance, adopt the intentional stance toward an inert object. We might explain the sedentary behavior of a flowerpot by saying that it wants to stay where it is and believes this is the best place for itself. Does this mean the flowerpot is an intentional agent? There are various ways in which interpretivism can avoid this unhappy result. For Davidson (1975), for instance, interpretability requires language. Creatures that are interpretable are those that use and interpret the language of others. According to Davidson, then, animals are not full-fledged thinkers and intentional agents. Some versions, however, most notably Dennett's, allow for the fact that the range of intentional systems will be quite large. It will range from very simple systems such as a thermostat to more complex agents such as ourselves. Interpretability, however, rests on the notion of explanatory adequacy. It is not just that one *can* take the intentional stance – attributing beliefs, intentions, and desires – but that doing so is explanatorily powerful. In the case of the flowerpot we have a system that does not exhibit a complex pattern of behavior. The intentional stance is not needed. The physical or design stance is more powerful.

According to interpretivism, then, propositional attitudes such as belief are not internal states of the mind or brain but states of whole systems. Our practice of making sense of others by positing these dispositions involves taking the intentional stance and attributing attitudes according to the norms of rationality and with the reflexive constraint of intelligibility in mind. Rather than start with a list of criteria that a subject has to meet in order to be an intentional agent, interpretivism starts with our practice. It takes as its starting point the explanatory power of this practice. If we are able to understand and predict the behavior of a system using the intentional stance, then we have every reason to believe we are dealing with one.

2 Groups as Intentional Systems

This brief discussion of intepretivism will have to suffice.[4] I want to turn now to consider how interpretivism can be extended to understand our practice of making sense of groups. According to interpretivism, mental states are not states of the head or brain but states of the whole agent or system. They are dispositional states in that they are defined in terms of what an agent will do, say, and think under certain circumstances. To believe that it is snowing is to be disposed to behave in certain ways under certain conditions and to form other intentional states related to those involving snow.

My proposal is that we think of group attitudes as dispositional states of groups. We are positing not internal states to the group but global and relational states. Let's return to our Israel example from the introduction. Israel believes that Syria used chemical weapons on its own people. To attribute such a belief to Israel is to attribute a dispositional state that can be characterized in terms of certain counterfactuals about what Israel will say and do and think in various circumstances. If Israel is asked the question "Does Syria have chemical weapons?" they will have their spokesperson say "yes" or issue a statement saying "yes." If the UN puts in place sanctions against Syria, Israel is likely to support them, and so on. If we found out that Israel actually issued a statement denying that Syria used chemical weapons, we would start to doubt the accuracy of our ascription.

When we attribute these dispositional states to groups, we are taking the intentional stance toward the group. We assume that the group has a unified perspective – a rational point of view – and that it shares our norms of rationality. Once the assumption of rationality and a rational point of view is in place, we attribute beliefs, intentions, and desires to groups in the same way we do to individuals. We ascribe those beliefs that a group ought to have if it wants to achieve its goals efficiently and given its function in the environment. We attribute desires in the same manner. And such attributions are made holistically as well. They presuppose other beliefs, goals, and intentions. These attributions are then the basis for explanation and prediction of the actions of groups.

Do we actually apply this method in our explanation of group behavior? That is, do we adopt the "intentional stance" when we try to make sense of groups? I think reflection on our everyday practice reveals that we do. Consider the following example. Suppose we want to explain the incidents of gunfire during a naval blockade. We read the official rules of engagement published to govern navy operations. These rules embody the navy's rational point of view. We can then explain why the navy sometimes fires at other ships. Under certain conditions, specified in its rules of engagement, the navy will fire at anyone it believes to have hostile intent.[5] Or consider the predictions we make about car companies. What will the Ford Motor Company do in response to the rise in gas prices? If Ford is rational, then it will act so as to maximize its profits. Because the company wants to avoid losing money on its line of large vehicles and believes that individuals are less likely to buy large vehicles during a time at which gas prices are high, we can predict that Ford will discount its large vehicles. Our practice of interpreting the actions of groups is just an extension of our practice of making sense of individuals, and it is governed by the same constitutive rules. If our assumption of rationality is justified in the case of groups, then this is good grounds for counting certain groups as intentional agents.

We don't always take the intentional stance toward groups, however, and not all groups will be the appropriate target of the intentional stance. In some cases, we might be dealing with a group of people whose agency is not unified enough to justify the assumption of a rational point of view. Or we might not be dealing with a group whose agency is extended over time in a way that makes their behavior complex enough to warrant the intentional stance. The design stance may be more appropriate. The explanatory power of the intentional stance constrains which groups count as intentional agents. An organization is the paradigm case of a group that is usefully made sense of from the intentional stance. The structure of an organization allows for complex behavioral patterns to arise and the synthesizing of individual perspectives into a unified perspective.

But is our practice of explaining and predicting the actions of groups in terms of beliefs, desires, and intentions explanatorily powerful? We discussed the issue of explanatory power briefly in chapter 4. There are a variety of explanatory projects that might motivate the need to take the intentional stance toward groups. We want to explain not only token group actions but types of group actions. I also suggested that, if one takes too stringent a notion of explanation, we run the risk of ruling out the beliefs and intentions of individuals as explanatory of individual human action and lots of other seemingly useful explanations in everyday contexts. I want to add here that taking the intentional stance, toward individuals and toward certain groups, allows us to see patterns we might not otherwise see if we adopt merely the design or physical stance.

Interpretivism is a "mild and intermediate sort of realism" (Dennett, 1991, p. 29). The patterns of human behavior discernible from the intentional stance are objectively out there to be interpreted. In "Real patterns" (1991) Dennett develops this point more fully. He appeals to Gregory Chaitin's definition of mathematical randomness: "A series (of dots or numbers of whatever) is random if and only if the information required to describe (transmit) the series accurately is incompressible: nothing shorter than the verbatim bit map will preserve the series. Then a series is not random – has a pattern – if and only if there some more efficient way of describing it" (Dennett, 1991, p. 32). A pattern, then, is real if there is a description of the data that is more efficient than the bit map. There may, of course, be several different ways to describe the data efficiently, but that fact does not mean that the pattern is not really out there to be described.

Dennett applies these considerations to the arena of intentional state attribution. The patterns of human behavior are real patterns because there is a description of human behavior that is more efficient than a description that cites microphysical properties. The more efficient description is the one offered at the level of folk psychology. It is only from the intentional stance that we can discern these real patterns. There may be several ways of interpreting an agent, each equally successful, but this fact does not mean that the patterns are any less real. We can extend Dennett's point to groups. The interpretative stance we take toward groups is able to discern real patterns of social behavior, patterns that are missed if one attempts to explain the social world by appealing only to individual intentional states.

Imagine that two people are engaging in a prediction contest. Their task is to predict what the Ford Motor Company will do in response to the enormous increase in gas prices. One of the participants is a methodological individualist. He is certain that social phenomena can be explained and predicted by appealing to individual intentional states. The other is a collectivist, and she believes that predicting the behavior of an organization involves viewing the organization as a rational agent. In order to predict what Ford will do, the individualist will have to find out who the operative members of the organization are, how each member voted and why they voted that way, and whether they are telling the truth about their intentional states. The collectivist, on the other hand, knowing that individuals are likely to stop buying large vehicles during a time when gas prices are high, and knowing that Ford sells a great deal of these vehicles and wants to continue to maximize its profits, will predict that Ford will discount these vehicles in the near future. The prediction is a bit risky, perhaps, but a pretty good one nonetheless. The individualist may make the same prediction, but he will have expended a considerable amount of time and energy. Compared to that of the individualist, the collectivist's performance will look like magic. How did she know Ford would lower its prices on large vehicles without even talking to the president of the company? There are real patterns that emerge from interactions of individuals that require for their interpretation the intentional stance.

Interpretivism, then, allows us to be "mild and intermediate" realists about the intentional states of groups. Groups and individuals really have mental states, but their ontological status is more akin to centers of gravity than tables and chairs. Bryce Huebner (2014) has argued that an interpretivist approach to group mental states is methodologically inert.

> Even if positing mental state facilitates reliable predictions of group behavior, this fact on its own should not persuade anyone who is not already a dyed-in-the-wool instrumentalist that there are group mental states or processes. The sort of instrumentalism required to infer group mentality from the predictability of group behavior yields an implausibly promiscuous ontology of mind. So, the fact – if it is a fact – that the intentional stance can be used to interpret group behavior yields an argument against relying on the intentional stance as much as it yields an argument in favor of macrocognition [Huebner's term for group cognition]. (2014, p. 37)

Huebner insists that a defense of group cognition must turn to issues of the causal mechanisms that implement group mental states and processes.

There are several things to say here in response. First, regarding the burden of proof, Huebner seems to think that, in order to show that groups have mental states and cognitive processes, we must argue that a representational theory of mind can extend to groups. Starting with interpretivism won't help, according to Huebner, because only a "dyed-in-the-wool instrumentalist" will be persuaded. The fact that interpretivism extends to groups might be seen as an argument against interpretivism rather than an argument for group agency. It is true that I have not argued for interpretivism here. But it is also true that the fact – if it is a fact – that homuncular functionalism can extend to certain types of groups could very well be as much an argument against homuncular functionalism as for it. Although representationalism is a popular view in the philosophy of mind, there is by no means a consensus about its truth, and the variety Huebner offers is one of many others. It isn't clear to me that

Huebner is in a methodologically superior place. It is important to note, too, that the form of interpretivism I present is not a naïve instrumentalism. As we have seen, the intentional stance is able to see real patterns – patterns that cannot be discerned from either the design or the physical level.[6]

Huebner explores the ways the tools of cognitive science can and should be utilized to make sense of group behavior. But the theory of mind he adopts leads him to dispel with group belief and intention. But then we are left with an error theory regarding our practice of ascribing these states to groups. Strictly speaking, any explanation in terms of group mental states and processes will be false. Given the ubiquity of this practice in everyday contexts, in legal contexts, and in the context of social scientific research, I find this unacceptable.

Finally, Huebner's passage references a general worry about the ontological promiscuity of interpretivism. After all, according to some interpretivists, even a thermostat turns out to be an intentional system of a rudimentary sort. Huebner's point is that the intentional stance is too coarse grained to discriminate between real intentionality and *as if* intentionality, and hence too coarse grained to distinguish between genuine group mentality and cases where the behavior can be explained by appeal to individual attitudes and some aggregative function.

There are ways, however, to understand the notion of "interpretability" that make the intentional stance a much more fine-grained tool. Davidson (1975), for instance, fleshes out the notion of interpretability in terms of linguistic intelligibility. Of course, this way of doing so might be too fine grained, as it puts animals outside the class of intentional agents. But it suggests that there are means of drawing boundaries by appreciating the ways in which the ascriptions we make are embedded in rich interpretive practices – practices that hold others epistemically and morally responsible, for instance. Our practice of making sense of others involves more than one-off ascriptions made to figure out what a system will do next. It involves rich narratives that position the subject within the realm of intelligibility. We don't just predict and explain the behavior of others; we attempt to *understand* them. Attributing attitudes to lecterns and dots moving across a page are no more examples of *using* the intentional stance than swinging a golf club is an example of playing golf. Huebner argues that the intentional stance on its own would not be able to discriminate between genuine cases of group mentality and cases where the behavior is simply a result of individual aggregative behavior. But this is too quick. I suspect that, if one really looked at attempts to explain the behavior of these groups, say in the context of an investigation into the legal culpability, we would find that the intentional stance breaks down at some point precisely in cases where there is no unified perspective of the group. Not all groups will turn out to be intentional agents on my approach.

But it is important to note that an interpretivist account of group agency is not necessarily in conflict with the accounts developed by Huebner and List and Pettit.[7] To see this we need to return to consider interpretivism and its relation to cognitive science. According to interpretivism, the subject of propositional attitude ascription is a whole system. What makes something an intentional agent is that its overall behavioral profile can be usefully interpreted from the intentional stance. But this is compatible with various ways in which this behavioral profile is generated. It might be generated, for instance, by the sort of computational mechanisms Huebner (2014) describes, or it might be generated by other cognitive architectures (connectionist, for instance). Dennett is careful to distinguish the question of what makes something an intentional system from the question of how the system generates the behaviors that justify attributions of intentionality (Dennett, 1987, pp. 43–4).

Likewise, I think we should distinguish between what makes a group an agent and what mechanisms generate the behaviors that justify the attributions of intentionality. Given the various types of groups in the world, their behavior will be generated in various ways. List and Pettit provide one such way – through the aggregation of votes – but we might imagine it being generated through consensus-building as well. It seems plausible that joint commitments or we-intentionality might also be part of the mechanisms that give rise to the complex behavior of groups such as corporations and organizations. Even the complex and detailed theories of methodological individualists such as Seumas Miller (2010) might be viewed as providing an account of the mechanisms that generate group behavior. This suggests, too, that such theories ought to be empirically informed, as the question of which mechanisms produce the complex behavior that is interpretable from the intentional stance cannot be discerned from the armchair. The sort of empirical work that we surveyed in the last chapter provides us with an account of how group agency arises in the *real* world.

3 Taking Stock

In this chapter I have laid out an alternative approach to group agency that starts with our practice of interpreting others. I began with an account of interpretivism. According to interpretivism, if a system exhibits complex behavioral patterns that can successfully be interpreted from the intentional stance, then we have every reason to believe we are dealing with an intentional agent. This isn't merely an epistemological theory about what we need to know about an agent in order to ascribe propositional attitudes to it; this is a substantive theory about the nature of mental states. Propositional attitudes are not internal states of a system but dispositional states of whole systems. Our practice of making sense of others involves positing these dispositions according to certain normative constraints (i.e., rationality). This view is consistent with a science of the mind which identifies the mechanisms that gives rise to such dispositions.

The benefits of this approach are threefold. First, by making the distinction between what intentional agency is and the mechanisms that implement it, we are able to acknowledge the fact that our practice of making sense of others, including groups, functions quite well without knowing anything about the "internal" mechanisms that might be responsible for the production of behavior that is interpretable from the intentional stance. Second, to the extent that approaches such as that of Huebner rest on a specific theory of the architecture of the mind, they are contingent, and their legitimacy hangs on whether or not that particular empirical theory turns out to be true. Interpretivism about group agency provides us with a theory that is not held hostage to developments in cognitive science but is consistent with them.[8] Finally, interpretivism offers us a moderate realism. It avoids having to say that our explanations in terms of group attitudes are systematically in error. Groups really do have attitudes, and our attributions are getting at real patterns in the world. We can acknowledge with skeptics that, if beliefs and intentions are stable, reidentifiable, internal states that serve as vehicles of intentional content, groups don't have these. Group beliefs and intentions are not real in that sense. But, as many have argued, it isn't clear whether individual propositional attitudes are real in this sense either.[9] Interpretivism is as real as it is going to get.

If we view our practice of making sense of certain groups as agents as an extension of our practice of making sense of others, then the attitudes we regularly ascribe to certain groups are to be identified not with sets of individual attitudes that are interrelated in various ways but with dispositional states of the whole group. Our practice of attributing such dispositional states is guided by norms of rationality and its attendant assumption of a rational point of view. If taking the intentional stance toward a group allows us usefully to understand the group's actions, then we have every reason to believe our assumptions of rationality are justified and that we are dealing with an intentional agent.

4 Suggestions for Further Reading

For a very compelling defense of interpretivism, see Mölder (2010), and for a useful discussion of forms of interpretivism, see Haugeland (1998). Those interested in learning more about dispositionalism should start with Gilbert Ryle's seminal work *The Concept of Mind* (1949). For a more contemporary version of dispositionalism, see Baker (1995).

5 Questions for Discussion

1 What is the difference between interpretivism and the theories of mental states we surveyed at the beginning of chapter 4?

2 Do we take the intentional stance toward groups? If so, what kind of groups, and is it useful to do so?
3 What would taking the design or physical stance toward a group involve?
4 What is the difference between the approach to group agency offered in this chapter and the approaches we discussed in chapters 3 and 4? Which approach is more plausible?
5 According to some forms of interpretivism, thermostats are rudimentary intentional systems. Is this counterintuitive? Does mentality come in degrees?

6
The Moral Responsibility of Groups

In this chapter we will consider the question of whether a group (a corporate group in the sense defined in the introduction) can be held morally responsible for its actions. Let's begin by distinguishing the issue of group responsibility from another important and interesting phenomenon – shared responsibility. To illustrate the difference, consider a case where several individuals dump a small amount of toxin into a stream. We can imagine that no one individual's contribution polluted the stream but that each individual's contribution, when added to all the others, produced a polluted stream. The intuition is that they polluted the stream (who else could have?) but yet no one individual seems responsible for polluting it. One way to explain the sort of responsibility in question is to say that each individual *shares* responsibility for polluting the stream; each somehow gets a piece of the responsibility pie.[1] Group responsibility refers to the possibility that the group itself, rather than (or in addition to) the individuals within it, is the bearer of responsibility. The question facing us in this chapter is whether group responsibility is a plausible notion. Are group agents moral agents?

1 Some Reasons for Attributing Moral Responsibility to Groups

We can begin by considering some reasons for attributing responsibility to groups. We have a rich practice of attributing moral responsibility to individuals, and if there are ways of distributing moral responsibility to individuals in a group in order to account for shared responsibility (as I described above), then what reason do we have for attributing moral responsibility to a group? We might call this the non-residual problem: once all the individual responsibility is attributed, what is left over to give to the group? One way to respond to this problem is to argue that the attribution of group responsibility allows for group-based harms to be addressed when the attribution of individual responsibility is impossible (because not every individual intended the harm) or there is no tractable way to determine individual contributions to the harm. Imagine a loosely organized terrorist network whose members all contribute to a large-scale terrorist attack. We can imagine that some of these members intended the harm but others may have been unaware of what their actions were contributing to. We can also imagine that there is no way to tell exactly who contributed what and how each individual's actions contributed to the attack (perhaps it was a cyber-attack, the details are complicated, and the contributions were diffuse and over long periods of time), and so there is no way to attribute responsibility to each person. According to this line of reasoning, in these cases we ought to attribute responsibility to the group as a whole, otherwise harms go unaddressed.[2] Do we want to say that no one is responsible for the terrorist attack? For practical reasons we need to attribute responsibility to someone in these cases, and so the group, as a whole, should be the target. But this approach leaves unanswered the original question, "But are groups *really* morally responsible?" This approach argues that the practice of *holding* groups responsible is justifiable on practical grounds, but it doesn't answer the question of whether groups *are* responsible.

One might argue that in cases where there are actions that can be done only by groups, attributions of responsibility are required.[3] The requirement is not a mere practical requirement but a normative one. That is, without such attributions we miss something from the moral order and we fail to pick out morally salient properties. Consider the case of genocide. Genocide isn't an act that can be perpetrated by an individual. No individual can commit genocide. Rather, genocide is a group act. It is something that groups do. Individuals contribute to genocide by committing various individual actions, but their contributions are not themselves genocide. But surely genocide is a morally culpable act so, if no individual is capable of committing genocide, we must, in order to be able to acknowledge the moral valence of the action, attribute responsibility to the group (the nation, tribe, etc.).[4] Further, the actions of individuals have a different moral significance when they contribute to the action of a group that is morally culpable.[5] Consider again the case of genocide. If Rose goes to her neighbors' house and kills all of its inhabitants, this action will have a different moral significance if it is part of a larger plan to wipe out a certain group of people to which Rose's neighbors belong. This seems clear in cases where an individual act of violence is found to be part of a terrorist plot. The moral significance of the individual action depends, in part, on the immorality of the group or group action.[6] So there seem to be reasons for acknowledging the group itself, in some cases, as the bearer of moral responsibility. But how is this possible?

2   The Metaphysics of Group Moral Responsibility

In chapters 3, 4, and 5 we considered various ways to make the case for group intentional agency. It might seem, then, an easy task to establish that groups are morally responsible. But we can't just move from intentional agency to moral agency or from cognitive systems to moral actors. Animals, for instance, are intentional agents and cognitive systems, but they are not morally responsible for their actions. Likewise, sophisticated robots might be simple intentional and cognitive systems, but we don't hold them morally responsible.

Perhaps, then, what is required for moral responsibility is personhood. This way of specifying the criterion for moral responsibility poses a challenge for accounts of group moral responsibility. Personhood is often associated with self-consciousness and self-reflection. Groups, according to many, don't have these features. They are not persons and so cannot be held morally responsible.

There are various ways one might respond to this challenge. One might argue that some groups meet the conditions for personhood. This is, in fact, an argument Peter French defended in 1979 in an article entitled "The corporation as a moral person." In that article French argues that corporations exhibit intentionality, are capable of exhibiting rationality, and are capable of being responsive to reasons and altering their behavior in light of reasons. Critics charge French with anthropomorphism and maintain that persons, unlike corporations, are ends in themselves.[7]

A second way to avoid the personhood objection is to acknowledge that groups are persons not in the sense that human beings are but in a different sense. This is the approach taken by List and Pettit (2012), who make a distinction between the intrinsic notion and the performative sense of personhood. Human beings are intrinsic persons, but moral agency requires the performative sense of personhood. To be a person in the performative sense is to be granted a certain normative status by members of the community. Infants, though intrinsic persons, are not persons in the performative sense. Certain types of groups, according to List and Pettit, meet the conditions for performative personhood.

Finally, a third way to respond to worries about personhood is to argue that personhood is not required for the attribution of moral responsibility. French takes this route in more recent work. He revised his theory and argues that, although they are not persons, groups are moral actors. Moral actors have rationality and intentionality and in addition are responsive to the demands (or reasons) of a moral community. French argues that corporations meet these criteria despite the fact that they are not persons.

Tying moral responsibility to personhood doesn't seem to help us move the debate further, however. It just pushes the question back one step further. We want to know what it is about certain creatures that makes it possible to hold them morally responsible. If we call those creatures "persons," that doesn't help us answer the question. The question then just becomes "What is it about persons that makes it possible to hold them morally responsible?" French's attempt to identify some sufficient conditions for moral responsibility (intentionality, rationality, and reasons-responsiveness) seems like a better move.

But what does it mean to be responsive to normative demands and what does such responsiveness require? Paul Sheehy (2006)[8] has argued that, in order for an agent to respond to moral demands, they need to possess the capacity for self-reflection and deliberation. A moral agent needs to be able to consider their values, goals, and actions and to evaluate those values, goals, and actions according to normative standards. Although many groups do not have such a capacity, Sheehy argues that some are capable of reflecting on their goals, character, and practices and as such are capable of bringing about change in response to normative demands. A group reflects upon itself and deliberates about its character through its individual members. Consider the case of a university that has been accused (perhaps both in the legal context and in the public arena) of not taking allegations of sexual harassment seriously. The university can reflect on its character by forming a committee to review policy on sexual harassment and the ways in which the school deals with allegations. The members of the committee would deliberate from the we-perspective or the we-mode by considering the perspective of the university.[9]

In addition to the capacity for deliberation and reflection, moral responsibility requires the ability to choose freely. According to many philosophers, if an agent is not capable of choosing otherwise, they are not free. The issue here is one of control. If a person is not in control, they cannot be held morally responsible. Imagine you are driving a car and the brakes stop working. You do all you can to avoid running into someone, but inevitably you crash into a local café and several people are harmed. You could not have done otherwise (we can imagine that you didn't have any options for crashing into something without people being harmed). The control requirement is explicitly acknowledged in List and Pettit's account of how groups can be held morally responsible. According to List and Pettit, in order for a group agent to be held responsible, it must:

i)   face a moral choice, that is, when it faces the choice of doing something good or bad, moral or immoral;

ii)   have a decision-making capacity to consider the evidence for and against certain morally significant actions;
iii)   have "the control required for choosing between options." (2011, p. 158)

The control condition, however, gives rise to the control problem. List and Pettit focus a great deal of time on trying to solve the control problem. Here is how they formulate it:

1   Whatever a group agent does is done by individual agents.
2   Individuals are in control of anything they do, and so in control of anything they do in acting for a group.
3   One and the same action cannot be subject both to the control of the group agent and to the control of one or more individuals.

Therefore,

4   The group agent cannot be in control of what it does.
5   Therefore, a group agent cannot be held morally responsible for its actions. (Ibid., p. 160)

List and Pettit's response to this argument involves appeal to their distinction between programming and implementing causes, which we considered in chapter 4: the sense in which groups are in control is the sense in which the boiling temperature programs for the flask to break. Groups can program for certain effects even though those effects are ultimately brought about by the actions of individuals.

The accounts of group moral responsibility we have discussed so far begin with criteria of moral agency and responsibility and show how certain groups could meet those criteria. Another approach would be to start with our practice of morally praising and blaming groups and see what this reveals about the conditions for moral responsibility.[10] We praise our sports teams, our school districts, and our non-profit organizations. We blame corporations, governments, and institutions. A striking example of our practice, in both scope and depth, is the discourse surrounding tobacco companies. In 1994 a box containing several thousand pages of internal documents from the Brown & Williamson Tobacco

Corporation arrived at Professor Stanton Glantz's office. It was a surprise to him and to the tobacco industry as well. Professor Glantz is a member of the institute for Health Policy Studies and the Department of Medicine at the University of California, San Francisco. He has long studied the effect of cigarette smoking on health and the impact the tobacco industry has had on health policy. Called *The Cigarette Papers* (Glantz, 1996), these documents had the same effect as the Pentagon papers on discussions of the Vietnam War and provided a key insight into the mind of an institution. They showed evidence of the tobacco companies' knowledge of the harms of tobacco and their extended campaign to suppress and alter scientific evidence regarding the harms of cigarette smoking. Here is a quotation from the foreword to *The Cigarette Papers* from the former Surgeon General Everett Koop:

> In the course of my own annual press conferences on the release of the Surgeon General's reports to Congress, I frequently spoke of the sleazy behavior of the tobacco industry in its attempts to discredit legitimate science as part of its overall effort to create controversy and doubt ... This book reveals these campaigns from the inside out. Smokers and nonsmokers alike should feel misled by the tobacco companies and their deceptive practices. (1996, xiv)

Glantz's book has served as evidence in support of attributions of moral responsibility to the industry (and not just legal responsibility). The blame has been placed on the industry, not on particular persons within the industry, though there is some individual blame placed on them as well. What are we to make of this practice and what can reflection on our practice of praise and blame tell us about moral responsibility?

3 Our Practice of Moral Appraisal

The focus on practice is reminiscent of that taken by P. F. Strawson in "Freedom and resentment" (1968). In that paper Strawson is dealing with the issue of individual human responsibility. He doesn't deal with the issue of group responsibility at all. Indeed, he probably would have resisted such an idea. What he does is try to detach the issue of moral responsibility from the metaphysical issue of determinism. Determinism is the view that all human actions are determined and therefore not under the control of individuals. According to the determinist, there is no free will and therefore no moral responsibility. A great deal of ink has been spilled in trying to solve the apparent conflict between determinism and moral responsibility. Strawson suggests that, if we look at our practice of holding others responsible, we shall see that the issue of determinism isn't really relevant to whether the practice is justified or not.

Strawson argues that the *participant reactive attitudes* – attitudes such as resentment, gratitude, forgiveness, and so on – to which we are subject by virtue of our participation in certain interpersonal relationships provide the justification for holding individuals morally responsible. These reactive attitudes constitute moral responsibility. That is, to hold another responsible is just to be prone to have the appropriate reactive attitude toward them. Even if the thesis of determinism is true, this will not and should not overturn our practice of holding others responsible.

The reactive attitudes can be classified into three categories: the personal, the vicarious, and the self-reactive. The personal reactive attitudes are those attitudes we feel when either good will or ill will is shown to us (e.g., resentment, jealousy). The vicarious reactive attitudes are those attitudes we feel in response to ill will or good will shown to others (e.g., disapprobation and indignation). The self-reactive attitudes are attitudes directed at ourselves in response to how we treat others and ourselves. Guilt, for instance, is paradigmatically a response to our own actions.[11]

Because the practice of holding responsible is a natural fact of adult human social life, it requires, according to Strawson, no theoretical truth as a basis for its justification. Libertarians appeal for justification to the theoretical claim that, in order to hold a person responsible, one must be metaphysically free. Utilitarians appeal for justification to the claim that holding people morally responsible regulates human behavior. But this "overintellectualization" of our practices is a mistake, according to Strawson. The propriety of the reactive attitudes is not established by some independent notion of responsibility. The explanatory priority is the other way around. As Gary Watson puts it:

> It is not that we hold people responsible because they are responsible; rather the idea (our idea) that we are responsible is to be understood by the practice, which itself is not a matter of holding some propositions to be true, but of expressing our concerns and demand about our treatment of one another. Holding responsible is as natural and primitive in human life as friendship and animosity, sympathy and antipathy. It rests on needs and concerns that are not so much to be justified as acknowledged. (1987, p. 259)

Despite the fact that Strawson denies the need for an external, rational justification for our reactive attitudes, he does acknowledge that these attitudes have their own *internal* criteria of application, which can be identified by reflecting on two kinds of cases. In the first case, a person does something that normally would indicate a lack of good will toward another, but in the current circumstances there isn't a manifestation of such ill will. If a good friend walks by me without saying hello, I am likely to feel a bit of resentment. But if I find out that my friend didn't recognize me, I will excuse her behavior and alter my attitude. It would be inappropriate for me to feel resentment under those circumstances. I will refer to these sorts of cases as involving "local" excuses.[12] These "local" excuses inhibit the reactive attitudes.

In the second kind of case, we don't simply excuse a person but we exempt them. Very young children, the mentally deranged, the severely handicapped, and so on, are not appropriate targets of our reactive attitudes. Why is this? Following Lawrence Stern (1974) and Gary Watson (1987), we can say that what is missing in these cases is the potential for moral address. Membership in the moral community requires that the subject be a potential participant in interpersonal interactions. To the extent that very young children and others in "unfortunate formative circumstances" lack the capacity for moral address, they are not appropriate targets for our reactive attitudes and, therefore, not appropriate subjects of moral responsibility. We can say that in these cases there are "global"[13] considerations that exempt a subject from moral responsibility.

These local and global excuses provide us with guidelines for the appropriateness of the reactive attitudes and, in effect, with criteria for moral responsibility. We need not establish some theoretical claim about determinism or autonomous agency in order to attribute responsibility. Instead, attributions of responsibility are based on pragmatic considerations related to the local and global excuses mentioned above. We ask "Does her behavior exhibit ill will?" or "Is she capable of moral address?" If the answer to either one of these questions is "no," then the reactive attitudes are not appropriate and the ascription of moral responsibility misplaced.

When we exempt another from moral responsibility on a long-term basis, as we do with the mentally deranged, we take what Strawson calls the objective attitude toward the person, meaning that we treat the person as someone to be managed, directed, handled, cured, manipulated, and so on. One cannot, according to Strawson, have a mature relationship with an individual whom one views with an objective attitude. "If your attitude towards someone is wholly objective, then though you may fight him, you cannot quarrel with him, and though you may talk to him, even negotiate with him, you cannot reason with him. You can at most pretend to quarrel, or to reason, with him" (Strawson, 1968, p. 79). To view someone with an objective attitude, then, is to view them as outside the moral community.

The incompatibilist, in effect, says that, if determinism is true, we are required to adopt the objective attitude toward everyone; there is no difference between the actions of the mentally deranged or the severely handicapped and our actions as adult human beings. But in Strawson's view this is absurd. Given the role the reactive attitudes play in our lives we couldn't adopt a thoroughgoing objective attitude toward others and ourselves.

Further, Strawson argues that, in cases where we do adopt the objective attitude, it is not because we accept a general thesis about determinism. We do so either because there are circumstances that inhibit the attitudes or there are circumstances that justify exempting the subject from the demands of the moral community. Thus, the truth of determinism (if it is true) is completely compatible with our practice of holding people responsible.

Strawson's focus is on the attitudes we have toward individuals and ourselves. But we also have reactive attitudes toward groups. Consider, again, contemporary attitudes toward tobacco companies. Many, of course, are angry with people within the organization. But the anger is also directed at the tobacco companies. We do not reserve our reactive attitudes for individuals. We unleash our indignation and resentment on groups. The recent sex scandals plaguing the Catholic Church throughout America and elsewhere provide us with another example of how the target of our reactive attitudes is sometimes a group. Although much of the anger and resentment may be directed at the individuals who perpetrated the abuse, there is also anger and resentment directed at the Church itself because of the apparent cover-up of what was taking place. The continual mishandling of complaints, the feigning of ignorance and the reassigning of priests are acts of the Church; individuals acted on behalf of and in their role as representatives of the Church. Their individual actions were the manifestation of Church policy, and this policy seems to reveal a general disregard for the victims of sexual abuse. Our indignation on behalf of the victims is directed not just at the individuals who committed and participated in the cover-up but also at the institution that condoned it and, in certain cases, made it possible.

The reactive attitudes we have toward groups such as corporations need not be negative. We also may have positive attitudes toward them, such as gratitude and even, perhaps, love. Aren't we sometimes grateful for the support, moral or financial, of certain groups – scholarship foundations, juries, political action groups? Or consider the feelings some people have for sports teams. Although many fans love individual players, there also seem to be attitudes that are directed at the teams themselves. Indeed, many fans remain committed to their team despite the fact that the players, management, and even ownership change.

Faced with the fact that we do have reactive attitudes toward groups, we can now ask whether these attitudes are justified. Those skeptical of the notion of group responsibility will argue that these attitudes are never justified. Getting angry with a tobacco company is like getting angry with one's pet or the table on which one stubs a toe. I am not justified in resenting the table that met my foot because the table is not a moral agent – a person – and reactive attitudes are appropriately directed only at persons. Likewise, according to the skeptic, we are not justified in having reactive attitudes toward groups because groups are not moral persons.

Now one might respond to this sort of skepticism as French does by developing an account of personhood and extending it to groups. I think, however, that Strawson provides us with a much easier response. This sort of skepticism presupposes that the only way our reactive attitudes toward groups could be rationally justified is by appeal to some metaphysical fact about the status of groups as persons. But to look for a metaphysical fact to justify our attitudes would be to commit the very mistake that the determinists or utilitarian compatibilists make when they attempt to justify our reactive attitudes toward individuals. Strawson reminds us that the framework of the reactive attitudes is a given – "as a whole, it neither calls for, nor permits, an external 'rational' justification" (1968, p. 23). The only justification we can give for these attitudes is pragmatic and is *internal* to the structure of the reactive attitudes.

Reflecting on cases in which our reactive attitudes are intuitively inappropriate reveals the internal justification for our reactive attitudes toward individuals. Recall that there are "excusing" conditions that inhibit or modify the reactive attitudes. If I find out that my friend was suffering from temporary blindness as she walked past me, I should not feel resentment at her unfriendly behavior. There are also "exempting" conditions. These are cases where the subject is not capable of moral address – for instance, very young children, the severely handicapped, the mentally deranged, etc. These subjects require that we adopt the objective attitude toward them. The lack of ability to engage in a certain type of discourse precludes these subjects as appropriate targets of the reactive attitudes. As Watson (1987) puts it:

> The reactive attitudes are incipient forms of communication, not in the sense that resentment et al. are usually communicated;

very often, in fact, they are not. Rather, the most appropriate and direct expression of resentment is to address the other with a complaint and a demand. Being a child exempts, when it does, not because expressing resentment has no desirable effects; in fact, it often does. Rather, the reactive attitudes lose their point as forms of moral address. (1987, p. 265)

Given these exempting and excusing conditions, we can now return to the question of whether groups *themselves* are the appropriate targets of reactive attitudes. What are the excusing conditions at the level of the group? Well, surely there will be cases where a group action does not exhibit ill will or good will because it was, for instance, compelled. Suppose a branch of a company is forced by its parent company to institute a series of layoffs. Because the layoffs are necessitated by outside forces, the branch does not seem to be an appropriate target of our reactive attitudes. There will also be cases where a group is not the appropriate target of our reactive attitudes because the appropriate target is an individual or set of individuals. Consider the case of a philosophy department that fails to make a tenure track offer to one of its adjunct faculty even though it had led the young philosopher to think an offer would be forthcoming. If we find out that the Dean refused (despite earlier promises) to fund a tenure track position, our anger at the department would seem misplaced and inappropriate. It would be more appropriate to direct our anger at the Dean. So it seems that there will be various cases that constitute excusing conditions for groups.

But could organizations and other sorts of groups be excused all the time? That is, are they, like the mentally deranged, exempt? To ask this is to ask whether groups such as corporations meet the criterion we find implicit in the exempting conditions. That is, are groups capable of moral address? To answer this question we need to get clear on the notion of moral address and what the capacity for moral address entails. As Watson says, the reactive attitudes are really a form of "incipient communication." What does an agent have to have in order to be a participant in this sort of communication? This brings us back to the issue of reasons-responsiveness and self-reflection.

Prima facie, the agent must be able to understand the moral demands that are placed upon them. Further, there must be present in the agent the capacity to guide their behavior and attitudes in light of these moral demands. If the capacity to direct one's actions in light of reasons were lacking, moral address would be futile. The reasons one provided would never result in the alteration of action and attitude. The capacity to guide one's behavior and attitudes in light of moral demands, in turn, requires the capacity for deliberation. Agents must be able to attain some conformity between their values and their actions. And this conformity cannot come about in any old manner. Conformity secured by electric shock does not involve deliberative capacities. Conformity must be achieved by an act of reflection. The capacity for moral address, therefore, presupposes what John Doris has called normative competence – "a complex capacity enabling the possessor to appreciate the normative considerations, ascertain information relevant to particular normative judgments, and engage in effective deliberation" (2002, 136).

Do groups such as corporations have this capacity? One way to answer this question is to reflect on judgments of normative competency at the individual level. How do we determine if an individual has the capacity for normative competence? Well, we figure out if an agent has normative competency by starting the conversation. If the dialogue gets off the ground, if the agent engages in the practice of giving and taking reasons, responds to criticism, and so on, then we have very good reason to believe that the individual has that capacity. Anyone who has tried to reason with a ten-month-old child will have good evidence that the child lacks normative competency. The conversation is always one way. If we provide the child with reasons at all, it is not in order to provide him or her with additional fodder for the deliberative mill. We want the child to change his or her behavior, but we don't think the change will occur via complex deliberative processes that assess and evaluate reasons. Our interactions with very young children resemble Strawson's objective stance. Our aim in addressing the child is to shape his or her behavior. The conversation, if there is one at all, is a pretense.

In order to answer the question of whether groups have the capacity for moral address, then, we can simply ask whether we engage in dialogue with them. I think it is obvious that we do. We bring them to court, we file complaints, we address them in public forums, in the boardroom, before Congress. We, as Watson describes it, "address them with a complaint and a demand." Although we might talk to individual spokespeople, we intend in many cases to address the corporation itself. We communicate that it has failed to meet the *moral* demand, the demand to be treated with a modicum of good will and respect.

In May of 2002, Abercrombie & Fitch, a large clothing retail firm that targets consumers aged seven to twenty-one, began selling thong underwear for young girls. The rear-less undergarments came in sizes for girls aged nine to sixteen. The smallest size appears to have been small enough to fit even younger girls. The thongs, some with the words "eye candy" and "wink, wink" printed on the front, were distributed to stores across the United States. Within two days the company was bombarded with emails and calls from parents. The first response from the company was defiant. Hampton Carney, spokesman for the company, said in an early interview that the company did not find the thongs for girls nine years and older morally objectionable. Mr Carney, speaking without much personal authority, claimed that there are "100 reasons why a young girl would want thong underwear," including the "need" to hide "visible panty lines." Conservative groups and feminists groups were not convinced. Complaints continued to inundate the corporate offices. The thongs were eventually removed from the sales floor and the company released this statement: "The underwear for young girls was created with the intent to be lighthearted and cute. Any misrepresentation of that is purely in the eye of the beholder."

This is hardly an admission of a moral lapse. Indeed, the company maintains that it did nothing wrong. But one need not be persuaded by moral reasons in order to be a participant in an exchange of reasons. There was deliberate reflection concerning the product and its relation to the company's commitments and aims. Abercrombie & Fitch are known for their risky marketing campaigns. They have been repeatedly accused of sexualizing young children. It may be one of their aims to play on this controversy in order to bring their products more recognition. The ultimate withdrawal of the offending undergarments from shelves was a result of a great deal of deliberation about how this would affect the company. Whatever the motive, the accusations clearly fall into the moral domain. And feminists and conservatives are not simply trying to "manage, handle, cure, or train" this company. Their letters are attempts to reason with the company.

This giving and taking of reasons occurs all the time in corporate contexts, particularly in discussions of corporate character. Consider the ways in which tobacco companies have attempted to persuade us that they are not so bad after all. Kraft, owner of R. J. Reynolds Tobacco, has produced hundreds of television commercials that show how the company provides aid to victims of floods and other natural disasters. The company's actions in this domain are supposed to stand as reasons in the conversation our culture is having concerning their moral worth. That such a dialogue occurs is strong evidence that these companies and other such groups have the capacity for moral address. For how else would this dialogue get off the ground?

This distinctively third-person approach is likely to be met with skepticism. If we do engage in discussion with groups, the skeptic will say, it is only because the group is made up of individuals with the capacity for moral address. Thus, the fact that we engage in dialogue with a group is not evidence that the group *itself* has the capacity. Individuals do the deliberating and talking, not groups, according to this objection.

I think this skepticism fails to understand the complex nature of social institutions, the ways in which authority structures and roles transform individual actions into group actions and the distinct properties that arise at the group level. First, although we engage in dialogue with institutions *through* their members, these members are speaking, in many cases, on behalf of the company. Given their role and the structure of the institution, their words are the words of the company. Second, as we have seen, groups themselves deliberate. They engage in the same deliberative processes in which individuals engage; they propose solutions, consider means to ends, contemplate possible alternatives, provide critical reflection on possibilities, assess options, draw conclusions, and so on. These tasks are distributed in the context of group deliberation. One person might offer a solution, another evaluate it, yet another suggest an amendment to the original proposal, and so on. Group deliberation is distributed cognition. And group cognition has the potential to be a significantly more efficient process than individual deliberation. Thus, groups could actually have greater normative competency than individuals.

Third, the normative considerations that apply to a group may be different from those that apply to individuals. Consider the normative standards implicit in just war theory. These are standards that apply not to individuals – wars are not waged by individuals – but to military groups, governments, and so on. Although it is the individuals in the group that will have to appreciate these standards, their appreciation will be a function of their reflection on how the standard applies to the group, the group's actions, and themselves *qua* members.

Finally, as we have seen, normative competency involves the ability to ascertain relevant information in order to make normative judgments. In many cases a group will have a greater ability than an individual to ascertain relevant information. A distribution of labor will allow for more information to be collected and pooled together for reflection. And the different perspectives of individuals in the group will contribute to a multidimensional view of the information relevant to certain normative judgments. The different perspectives can also contribute to a more objective assessment of the situation and the moral demands. The point here is similar to those made by feminist philosophers of science. Objectivity comes through intersubjective criticism. It is only within the context of dialogue with others that the subjective biases that inhibit moral competency can be overcome.

No doubt some aspects of the normative competency of the group can be understood reductively. Normative competency involves the appreciation of norms. This appreciation is best understood in terms of the capacities of individual group members. But group members will appreciate norms *qua* group members. Outside of one's group these norms may not have any force for the individual *qua* individual. Further, in some cases these norms apply only at the group level. They govern group actions that in some instances cannot be understood reductively. Finally, some groups have the capacity to engage in joint deliberation. These deliberative processes do not consist merely of individuals engaging in deliberation alongside others. Distributed cognition is a property of groups. Group norms and distributed cognition suggest that we cannot understand the moral competency of the group simply in terms of the moral competency of the individual members. Group normative competency is an emergent property.

If certain groups have normative competency, then they are the appropriate targets of our reactive attitudes. If they are the appropriate targets of our reactive attitudes and, as Strawson has argued, the reactive attitudes are constitutive of moral responsibility, then our practice of holding groups morally responsible has been vindicated. To hold a corporation or other group morally responsible is simply to be prone to have the appropriate reactive attitudes toward them, and for a group to *be* responsible is for them to be subject to the appropriate attitudes.

4   Lingering Concerns

Normative competency is the capacity to appreciate normative considerations, ascertain relevant information, and engage in effective deliberation. To "appreciate" normative considerations is simply to acknowledge the role these considerations have in your life and how they affect your commitments. In the context of deliberation, a group can come to understand how certain moral demands affect its commitments and goals. But critics have argued that an appreciation of moral demands requires the capacity to care, and care is essentially a qualitative state, one had only by conscious agents. Since groups are not conscious, they cannot care and therefore cannot appreciate normative reasons (Haney, 2004).

A related objection is that, in order for groups to be the appropriate targets of our moral sentiments, they must themselves be capable of having reactive attitudes. To exhibit ill will or good will, according to this objection, presupposes the existence of certain sentiments. We exhibit ill will, for instance, when we are angry. But how could a group itself have reactive attitudes? These attitudes are emotions and emotions are feelings. How could the group, itself, *feel*?

I do not have space here to give this worry a thorough response, but let me make an attempt to diminish its force. First, it is not at all clear that in order to exhibit ill will or good will one must be capable of moral sentiments. Couldn't there be a creature which had evil aims without also having feelings such as hatred and resentment? But even if one must have reactive attitudes in order to be an appropriate target of the attitudes of others, there may be a legitimate sense in which groups can have reactive attitudes. Consider Margaret Gilbert's account of group remorse: "Group G feels remorse over an act A if and only if the members of G are jointly committed to feeling remorse as a body over act A" (2000, p. 135). Group remorse, according to this analysis, is a function of the joint commitment to form a unified subject that expresses remorse. Individuals *qua* members of the group will do what they can in terms of their actions and utterances to form such a subject.

Now one might argue that this is not an account of group remorse because there is no subject that "feels" remorse. But, as Gilbert points out, it is not at all clear that feelings are constitutive of the emotions.

> Consider the case of an individual human being. When I say to you "I feel great remorse," must I be saying something false unless there are pangs or the like in the background? On the face of it, I need not be saying something false. Note that some apparently equivalent expressions do not use the term "feel" at all: "I am full of remorse"; "I am truly remorseful." (2000, p. 135)

It might be argued, then, that the essential nature of emotion is to be characterized not in terms of qualitative feelings but in terms of judgments and other intentional states such as desires. The fact that groups lack feeling, then, does not mean that they lack the capacity for reactive attitudes.[14]

Even if we admit that feelings are essential to emotion, one could understand group emotions as those emotions that are expressed *through* the members *qua* group members. Group reactive attitudes would be differentiated on this approach from individual reactive attitudes in terms of the norms governing the relevant reactions. Certain emotional responses might be licensed for an individual only because of her group membership. They would also be differentiated in terms of their motivational upshot. The "pangs" of remorse you feel *qua* group member may lead you to undertake actions that you would not perform *qua* individual. Although this approach does not have the group *itself* feeling the emotion, it does identify a way in which emotions can be realized by a group. Perhaps this is all we need in order for groups to be appropriate targets of our reactive attitudes.

Many fear the notion of group responsibility because they fear that the individual will be let off the hook. But the approach I am putting forward does not establish a scapegoat. The practice of holding individuals responsible is here to stay, and we need not fear that it will be replaced by group responsibility. My view means there is more responsibility in the world, not less.

One might also object to the idea of group moral responsibility on the grounds that groups cannot be punished. This objection is related to the idea that groups cannot feel or have emotions. Just punishment seems to require a subject that is capable of feeling something – pain or anguish at the loss of losing their freedom or some other privilege. Punishment presupposes the capacity for suffering. We do, however, punish groups. We boycott them, dissolve them, and impose sanctions on them. We do so without concern about whether the group itself feels the pain of such punishment. But this raises a related concern: when an institution receives sanctions it is the members of the organization that suffer, not the group itself. This seems, according to this objection, unfair, especially to those members who did not contribute to the group action that was sanctioned.

The relationship between moral responsibility and punishment is complex, and I can't hope to address these objections in detail here. But one thing to consider is that, if we require the capacity for emotion in order to hold a person morally responsible and in order to punish them for violations to moral norms, we may end up having to exempt those whose emotional life is diminished or lacking to a severe degree. People with affective disorders (especially severe forms such as reactive attachment disorder) often fail to have the appropriate emotional responses to the actions of others and themselves. They simply cannot care in the ways that normal human beings do. Perhaps such people should not be held morally responsible? Perhaps we should simply count them as mentally ill and so not in control of their actions and morally culpable? This would preserve the intuition that punishment requires a sort of emotional capacity. But when we consider some of the people who are thought to have had severe emotional disorders (Ted Bundy, Hitler, Jeffrey Dahmer) it becomes difficult to see this as justified. These considerations also speak to the objection that rests on the idea that, in order to be morally responsible, you must be not simply the target of reactive attitudes but a subject of them as well. Such a view runs the risk of exempting from moral responsibility what many of us would describe as the truly evil person.

Finally, reflection on individual moral responsibility and punishment reveals that punishment of an individual can result in consequences for others that may seem unfair. The child whose father is convicted and sentenced to jail is punished in a way as well. This is certainly regrettable. The fact that some members of a group may suffer the consequences of group sanctions is an unfortunate consequence but not something that should question the legitimacy of our practice of sanctioning groups.

5 Taking Stock

I began this chapter with some reasons for taking group responsibility seriously. There are certain normative dimensions of social life that would be difficult if not impossible to capture without our practice of holding groups responsible. The motivations for acknowledging groups as full-fledged moral agents rests, in part, on what we might call the desire to "save the phenomenon." But why think that saving the phenomenon requires acknowledging groups as genuine moral agents? Aren't there ways to acknowledge our practice of holding groups responsible and the need for such a practice without positing genuine moral agency? Michael McKenna (2006) has suggested something of this sort. He argues that assigning *moral burdens* to a corporate agent need not require that we also attribute moral responsibility. The assigning of moral burdens is, according to McKenna, an issue for political philosophy, and "there is nothing controversial in holding that there are good reasons grounded in considerations of justice for requiring that certain institutions as opposed to others take on certain moral burdens" (2006, p. 31).

A similar move has been proposed by Mitch Haney (2004). Haney argues that corporate groups cannot be held morally responsible because moral responsibility requires the capacity for reactive attitudes, but there is a distinction between holding someone morally responsible and holding someone accountable. If, when my son was four, he climbed into my car with my keys and put them into the ignition, started the car, put it in reverse, and backed the car into the neighbor's car parked on the street in front of our driveway, I would have been held accountable. I would not be morally responsible for damaging my neighbor's car but I can be held accountable for my child's actions (and for leaving my keys around my precocious child). Likewise, Haney suggests that, although they cannot be held morally responsible, corporate agents can be held accountable. McKenna (2006) also suggests that there is a distinction between being morally responsible and holding someone morally responsible. Consider, again, my precocious four-year-old. Although I do not think that Riley, at the age of four, was capable of being held morally responsible, I would not have responded to his imagined behavior (though he did actually climb in the car with his brother one day with my keys and start the car; luckily I stopped them before they put it in gear) in a way devoid of moral assessment. I would have given him a "stern talking to," to say the least. That is, I would have treated him *as if* he were a morally responsible agent in order to foster his moral development. McKenna (2006) points out that we do this with addicts as well, though we know that their ability to control their own actions is often compromised. To treat them as if they are morally responsible agents provides them with the tools to develop the sense of self they need in order to take responsibility for their own lives. McKenna concludes, then, that, although metaphysically speaking corporate groups are not moral agents, there are good practical and political reasons for holding groups morally *accountable.*

Does such a position allow us to save the phenomenon? In particular, does it allow us to say that our reactive attitudes toward groups are justified? If our reactive attitudes are tracking not just moral responsibility but accountability and perhaps other morally salient features of actions and agents, then this approach would allow us to say that we are justified in our reactive responses to groups because such responses are appropriate responses to morally accountable subjects. Our practice of holding corporate groups responsible and responding to them with moral emotions is not to be dismissed as a silly error. Perhaps, then, we can save the phenomenon of our practice of holding responsible without having to acknowledge corporate groups as full-fledged moral agents. I am happy to accept such a compromise.

6   Suggestions for Further Reading

In addition to the texts cited above, those interested in delving deeper into the literature on group responsibility should look at the volume of *Midwest Studies* edited by Peter French and Howard Wettstein (2006) dedicated to shared and collective responsibility.

7   Questions for Discussion

1   What is the difference between shared responsibility and group responsibility? Is there any reason for attributing responsibility to a group?
2   Can one be a moral agent and lack all emotion?

3   Do we have reactive attitudes toward groups? Or are our emotions always targeted at people?
4   Is personhood required for moral agency?
5   What is the difference between moral responsibility and moral accountability?

Conclusion

In surveying the accounts of group belief and intention in chapters 1 and 2 we were able to identify a number of general features of belief and intention and how they might be realized in groups, and this led us to consider the functionalist approach to group agency and cognition in chapters 3 and 4. In chapter 5 I suggested that an interpretivist framework does a better job of showing how our practice of making sense of groups, a practice that I have argued is ubiquitous and explanatorily powerful (according to a broad notion of explanatory power), is justified. Even if one rejects the interpretivist framework, the basic insight that mental states are dispositional states of whole systems rather than internal, discrete states that carry informational content (as the neo-Cartesian would have it) provides a more easily extended account of propositional attitudes to groups. Finally, the issue of whether groups can be genuine moral agents was explored in chapter 6. Again I argue that we should put our practice at the forefront of such an investigation. But there were considerable objections to thinking that groups themselves could be the subject of the sorts of emotions that are constitutive of moral agency. In the end we may get only group accountability rather than group moral responsibility.

I'll be the first to admit the conditional nature of my theory. It rests on the truth of interpretivism. But I am not alone in having to rely on some theory of mind. Those of us arguing for genuine group agency have to start from some place, and, alas, there is no consensus in the philosophy of mind that would lend us a non-controversial starting point. Much of my argument rests on the explanatory power of appealing to group mental states and cognitive processes. Methodological individualists insist that such explanations are not powerful because there can always be an explanation of the phenomenon in terms of individual mental states and processes and their social settings. But a great deal of social science research is being done without explaining social phenomena in individualistic terms. The use of cognitive models to understand group behavior is growing, and the use of intentional idiom to explain group behavior is ubiquitous. In order to be able to say that these are not good explanations, one would need to provide an individualistic explanation to counter each of these group-level explanations and show that everything captured by the group-level explanation can be explained by the individualistic explanation. I have yet to see this done in any systematic way. Wilson (2004), for instance, hasn't provided a competing individualistic explanation of navigation on a naval vessel. Rather, he has just stated that there *is* an explanation that *could be* given at the individual level. Whether group-level explanations are powerful is an empirical question and will depend, in part, on the sorts of questions that are being asked in certain domains. In short, the jury is still out on the question of explanatory power.

If philosophers are like lawyers and ideas are our clients, then I rest my case. It is, as I noted, a difficult client to defend. This is partly because the theories of mind we have to work with are developed with the individual in mind. Extending accounts of individual minds to group minds might be a futile task. The point has often been made in debates about animal cognition and human minds. If you start with a conception of what it is to be minded that is focused exclusively on the adult human being, you may end up begging the question with respect to the possibility of other sorts of minds. Indeed, Gilbert (2002) has argued that insisting that groups are minded in the same ways as individuals are might ultimately cause us to miss something unique about the social case. But we need, it seems to me, to be able to say more about how group mental states might be similar enough to individual mental states to count as beliefs and intentions. I hope this book has gone some way toward doing that.

Notes

1 Group Belief

1 See Lewis (1969); Peacocke (2005); Ernst (2011).
2 Gilbert is likely to reply that it is not clear that other conversationalists have the standing to rebuke one another for violating the various Gricean norms unless a joint commitment is brought into the story somewhere. See her discussion of Scanlon's principle of fidelity (Gilbert, 2013, chap. 12).

2 Group Intention

1 Margaret Gilbert (1989, 2006) adopts a goal account of acting together which differs from that of Miller in significant ways; however, unlike Miller, she also gives an account of group intention. She believes both group goals and group intentions are needed in explaining the social world.
2 Miller (1995) has attempted to respond to this criticism.
3 A similar point was made against Margaret Gilbert's account of group belief in chapter 1. See Miller (2010) for a discussion of how his collective end theory is supposed to extend to institutions.
4 This is why I do not discuss we-beliefs in chapter 1. Raimo Tuomela appeals to we-beliefs in the context of a more complicated theory of group belief. We-beliefs could be the basis of a theory of group belief proper. I chose, however, to focus

on Tuomela's account of the belief of organizations because it best addresses the question of whether corporate groups have beliefs.

5 Bratman (2014) attempts to deal with this issue. To my mind it still comes up short, but I don't have space here to develop a detailed response.

6 Stoutland (2008) makes a similar distinction between plural agents and collective agents.

3 Group Agency

1 The vast majority of theories of propositional attitudes do not require that a subject be phenomenally conscious, and research on artificial intelligence would be defunct if consciousness was required for a system to exhibit intelligent behavior.

2 See Dennett (1987, 2011) for a defense of this view.

3 See Leo Townsend (2013) for a fuller articulation of this concern.

4 See also Szigeti (2014).

4 Group Cognition

1 Though this has by no means solved the problem of mental causation. It arises in a different form. Rather than debate whether an immaterial soul can move a material body, philosophers of mind debate whether what plays the causal role is the actual physical states of the brain or the mental properties of those physical states.

2 Although the identity theory lost momentum because of the problem of multiple realizability, it has recently made a comeback. Those who argue for the identity theory do so by rejecting multiple realizability. See, for instance, Polger (2009a, 2009b).

3 Clark actually argues that individual mental states are also epiphenomenal, and so we ought to understand ascriptions of beliefs to individuals as more akin to the issuing of corporate statements.

4 See Davidson (1963). Also, see Jaegwon Kim (1988) for a view motivated by the same sorts of causal worries.

5 John Biro (1981) and D. H. M Brooks (1986) also offer accounts of group minds/cognitive systems by extending functionalist accounts of mind.

6   Huebner (in correspondence) suggests that such ascriptions are tacit references to individuals *qua* group members or should be read distributively. This simply denies that we ever take the group itself to be the subject. I think this revises our practice considerably.

5   Interpreting Groups

1   This does not mean that in interpreting others we must assume that they believe everything that we believe or that we must always agree. Disagreements are inevitable. But disagreements are only possible against the backdrop of agreement.

2   In *The Bounds of Agency* (1998) Carol Rovane suggests a similar account of the notion of a rational point of view, which, she says, need not be tied to a particular soul, animal, or phenomenological viewpoint. A rational point of view is a view from which a person deliberates. According to Rovane, we engage in the following sorts of activities from the rational point of view: accept the implications of one's attitudes, resolve contradictions and conflicts, rank preferences, assess opportunities for action, determine means for arriving at ends, and consider the consequences of certain actions and attitudes. The rational point of view is essentially a normative notion. It is something in which contradictions and conflicts *ought* to be resolved, in which preferences *ought* to be weighed, etc. More generally, it is something from which, all things considered, judgments ought to be reached and implemented.

3   The notion of a rational point of view as a point of view from which certain cognitive activities proceed provides us with a much richer conception of rationality than can be found in either Dennett's or Davidson's discussion of interpretation. The norms of rationality require not just that our beliefs be consistent and mostly true but that we engage in certain activities that promote consistency and truth. Rationality, then, is not a state one reaches (i.e., the state of having all consistent beliefs) but an activity.

4   See Mölder (2010) and Zawidzki (forthcoming) for defenses of interpretivism.

5   This example is a version given by Clark (1994).

6   See Lynne Rudder Baker (1995) for a dispositional theory of propositional attitudes that is also a realist account.

7   List and Pettit mention the intentional stance in the first chapter of *Group Agency* (2011), and Tuomela's recent book (2013) makes reference to it as well.

8   Although it is held hostage to the truth of interpretivism, but interpretivism is not an empirical theory, and so we don't have to wait for science to progress in order to establish its merits.

9   See Zawidzki (forthcoming) for a discussion of the challenges facing neo-Cartesian approaches and a defense of Dennett.

6   The Moral Responsibility of Groups

1   See May (1996) for a defense of shared responsibility.

2   Larry May (1989) argues for this approach. His focus is on the actions of mobs, however, rather than corporate groups, but the same move could be made for corporate groups.

3   Tracy Isaacs (2006) argues in this way; the following example of genocide is hers. See also Isaacs (2011).

4   Methodological individualists resist this move. Miller (2010) has argued that the moral responsibility of genocide *can* be explained by appeal to individuals' contributions to the act and the fact that they are acting *as* group members.

5   Isaacs (2006) makes this point as well.

6   It should be noted that the methodological individualist will claim to be able to acknowledge this without having to posit responsibility at the group level.

7   See, for instance, Velasquez (1983), De George (1986), and Kerlin (1997).

8   Kay Mathiesen (2006) makes a similar move.

9   The distinction between the I-mode and the we-mode is discussed briefly in chapter 2.

10   I adopt this approach in "Participant reactive attitudes and collective responsibility" (2003), as does Silver (2005).

11   I say paradigmatically here because I leave open the possibility that there are group reactive attitudes. Group guilt may involve an attitude in response to a group action done by the group of which one is a member. I address the issue of group reactive attitudes briefly in section 3. See Gilbert (2002) for an insightful discussion of collective guilt.

12   I follow McKenna (1998) in this terminology.

13   Again, this is McKenna's terminology.

14   See Huebner (2011) for a defense of collective emotions.

References

Adams, F., and Aizawa, K. (2008) *The Bounds of Cognition.* Oxford: Blackwell.

Andric, Vuko (2014) Can groups be autonomous rational agents? A challenge to the List–Pettit theory. In Anita Konzelmann Ziv and Hans Bernhard Schmid (eds), *Institutions, Emotions, and Group Agents: Contributions to Social Ontology.* New York: Springer, pp. 343–53.

Anscombe, G. E. M. (1957) *Intention.* Cambridge, MA: Harvard University Press.

Armstrong, D. (1980) *The Nature of Mind.* Brisbane: University of Queensland Press.

Baier, A. (1997) Doing things with others: the mental commons. In L. Alanen, S. Heinämaa, and T. Wallgren (eds), *Commonality and Particularity in Ethics.* New York: St Martin's Press.

Baker, L. R. (1995) *Explaining Attitudes: A Practical Approach to the Mind.* Cambridge: Cambridge University Press.

Baltzer, U. (2002) Joint action of large groups. In Georg Meggle (ed.), *Social Facts & Collective Intentionality.* Frankfurt am Main: Hänsel-Hohenhausen, pp. 1–18.

Barnier, A., Sutton, J., Harris, C., and Wilson, R. (2008) A conceptual and empirical framework for the social distribution of cognition: the case of memory. *Cognitive Systems Research* 9(1–2): 33–51.

Biro, J. (1981) Persons as corporate entities and corporations as persons, *Nature and System* 3 (September): 173–80.

Bittner, R. (2002) An action for two. In Georg Meggle (ed.) *Social Facts & Collective Intentionality.* Frankfurt am Main: Hänsel-Hohenhausen.

Block, N. (2008) Phenomenal and access consciousness, *Proceedings of the Aristotelian Society* 108: 289–317.

Bratman, M. (1993) Shared intention, *Ethics* 104(1): 97–113.

Bratman, M. (2007) *Structures of Agency: Essays.* New York: Oxford University Press.

Bratman, M. (2014) *Shared Agency: A Planning Theory of Acting Together.* New York: Oxford University Press.

Brooks, D. H. M. (1986) Group minds, *Australasian Journal of Philosophy* 64(4): 456–70.

Cariani, F. (2012) Epistemology in group agency: six objections in search of truth, *Episteme* 9(3): 255–69.

Carruthers, P. (2006) *The Architecture of the Mind: Massive Modularity and the Flexibility of Thought.* Oxford: Clarendon Press.

Chalmers, D. J. (1996) *The Conscious Mind: In Search of a Fundamental Theory.* Oxford: Oxford University Press.

Chapman, B. (1998) Law, incommensurability, and conceptually sequenced argument, *University of Pennsylvania Law Review* 146: 1487–582.

Clark, A. (1994) Beliefs and desires incorporated, *Journal of Philosophy* 91(8): 404–25.

Clark, A. (2010) Memento's revenge: the extended mind revisited. In Richard Menary (ed.), *The Extended Mind.* Cambridge, MA: MIT Press, pp. 43–66.

Clark, A., and Chalmers, D. (1998) The extended mind, *Analysis* 58(1): 7–19.

Davidson, D. (1963) Actions, reasons, and causes, *Journal of Philosophy* 60(23): 685–700.

Davidson, D. (1973) Radical interpretation, *Dialectica* 27: 313–28.

Davidson, D. (1975) Thought and talk. In S. Guttenplan (ed.), *Mind and Language.* Oxford: Oxford University Press.

Davidson, D. (1978) *Essays on Actions and Events.* Oxford: Oxford University Press.

De George, R. (1986) Corporations and morality. In H. Curtler (ed.), *Shame, Responsibility and the Corporation.* New York: Haven, pp. 57–75.

Dennett, D. (1987) *The Intentional Stance.* Cambridge, MA: MIT Press.

Dennett, D. (1991) Real patterns, *Journal of Philosophy* 88(1): 27–51.

Dennett, D. (2011) Intentional systems theory. In B. McLaughlin, A. Beckermann, and S. Walter (eds), *The Oxford Handbook of Philosophy of Mind.* Oxford: Oxford University Press.

Doris, J. (2002) *Lack of Character: Personality and Moral Behavior.* Cambridge: Cambridge University Press.

Ernst, Z. (2011) What is common knowledge? *Episteme* 8(3): 209–26.

French, P. (1979) The corporation as a moral person. *American Philosophical Quarterly* 16(3): 207–15.

French, P. (1995) *Corporate Ethics*. Orlando, FL: Harcourt Brace.

Gilbert, M. (1987) Modelling collective belief, *Synthese* 73(1): 185–204.

Gilbert, M. (1989) *On Social Facts*. Princeton, NJ: Princeton University Press.

Gilbert, M. (1994) Remarks on group belief. In F. Schmitt (ed.), *Socializing Epistemology: The Social Dimensions of Knowledge*. Lanham, MD: Rowman & Littlefield, pp. 111–34.

Gilbert, M. (1996) *Living Together: Rationality, Sociality, and Obligation*. Lanham, MD: Rowman & Littlefield.

Gilbert, M. (2000) *Sociality and Responsibility: New Essays in Plural Subject Theory*. Lanham, MD: Rowman & Littlefield.

Gilbert, M. (2002) Collective guilt and collective guilt feelings, *Journal of Ethics* 6(2): 115–43.

Gilbert, M. (2006) *A Theory of Political Obligation: Membership, Commitment, and the Bonds of Society*. New York: Oxford University Press.

Gilbert, M. (2013) *Joint Commitment: How We Make the Social World*. New York: Oxford University Press.

Glantz, S. A. (1996) *The Cigarette Papers*. Berkeley: University of California Press.

Goldman, A. (ed.) (2012) Symposium on Christian List and Philip Pettit's *Group Agency*, *Episteme* 9(3).

Grice, P. (1975) Logic and conversation. In P. Cole and J. Morgan (eds), *Syntax and Semantics, 3: Speech Acts*. New York: Academic Press, pp. 41–58.

Hakli, R. (2007) On the possibility of group knowledge without belief, *Social Epistemology* 21(3): 249–66.

Haney, M. R. (2004) Corporate loss of innocence for the sake of accountability, *Journal of Social Philosophy* 35(3): 391–412.

Harris, C. B., Keil, P., Sutton, J., Barnier, A., and McIlwain, D. (2011) We remember, we forget: collaborative remembering in older couples, *Discourse Processes* 48(4): 267–303.

Haugeland, J. (1990) The intentionality all-stars, *Philosophical Perspectives* 4: 383–427.

Haugeland, J. (1998) *Having Thought: Essays in the Metaphysics of Mind*. Cambridge, MA: Harvard University Press.

Hollingshead, A. (1998) Retrieval processes in transactive memory systems, *Journal of Personality and Social Psychology* 74: 659–71.

Hollingshead, A., and Brandon, D. (2003) Potential benefits of communication in transactive memory systems, *Human Communication Research* 29: 607–15.

Huebner, B. (2011) Genuinely collective emotions, *European Journal for the Philosophy of Science* 1(1): 89–118.

Huebner, B. (2012) Review of *Group Agency: The Possibility, Design, and Status of Corporate Agents*, *Ethics* 122(3): 608–12.

Huebner, B. (2014) *Macrocognition*. Oxford: Oxford University Press.

Hutchins, E. (1991) The social organization of distributed cognition. In L. B. Resnick, J. M. Levine, and S. D. Teasley (eds), *Perspectives on Socially Shared Cognition*. Washington, DC: American Psychological Association, pp. 283–387.

Hutchins, E. (1995) *Cognition in the Wild*. Cambridge, MA: MIT Press.

Isaacs, T. (2006) Group moral responsibility and group intention. In P. French and H. Wettstein (eds), *Midwest Studies in Philosophy, 30(1): Shared Intentions and Collective Responsibility*. Malden, MA: Wiley-Blackwell, pp. 59–73.

Isaacs, T. (2011) *Moral Responsibility in Collective Contexts*. New York: Oxford University Press.

Jones, T. E. (2010) *What People Believe when They Say that People Believe: Folk Sociology and the Nature of Group Intentions*. Lanham, MD: Lexington Books.

Kerlin, M. J. (1997) Peter French, corporate ethics, and the Wizard of Oz, *Journal of Business Ethics* 16: 1431–8.

Kim, J. (1984) Epiphenomenal and supervenient causation, *Midwest Studies in Philosophy* 9(1): 257–70.

Kim, J. (1987) "Strong" and "global" supervenience revisited, *Philosophy and Phenomenological Research* 48: 315–26.

Kim, J. (1988) Explanatory realism, causal realism, and explanatory exclusion, *Midwest Studies in Philosophy* 12(1): 225–39.

Kornhauser, L. A., and Sager, L. G. (1986) Unpacking the court, *Yale Law Journal* 96: 82–117.

Kornhauser, L. A., and Sager, L. G. (1993) The one and the many: adjudication in collegial courts, *California Law Review* 81: 1–59.

Kutz, C. (2000) Acting together, *Philosophy and Phenomenological Research* 61(1): 1–31.

Lee, D. (2014) Job growth remains weak in January: unemployment rate falls to 6.6%, *Los Angeles Times*, February 7, www.latimes.com/business/money/la-fi-mo-january-jobs-report-20140207,0,823344.story#ixzz2seFWhPwZ.

Lewis, D. (1969) *Convention: A Philosophical Study*. Cambridge, MA: Harvard University Press.

Liang, D. W., Moreland, R. L., and Argote, L. (1995) Group versus individual training and group performance: the mediating role of transactive memory, *Personality and Social Psychology Bulletin* 21(4): 384–93.

List, C., and Pettit, P. (2011) *Group Agency: The Possibility, Design, and Status of Corporate Agents*. New York: Oxford University Press.

List, C., and Pettit, P. (2012) Episteme symposium on *Group Agency*: replies to Gaus, Cariani, Sylvan, and Briggs, *Episteme* 9(3): 293–309.

Mathiesen, K. (2006) We're all in this together: responsibility of collective agents and their members. In P. French and H. Wettstein (eds), *Midwest Studies in Philosophy, 30(1): Shared Intentions and Collective Responsibility*. Malden, MA: Wiley-Blackwell, pp. 240–55.

May, L. (1987) *The Morality of Groups: Collective Responsibility, Group-Based Harm, and Corporate Rights*. Notre Dame, IN: University of Notre Dame Press.

May, L. (1989) Mobs and collective responsibility, *Social Philosophy Today* 2: 300–11.

May, L. (1996) *Sharing Responsibility*. Chicago: University of Chicago Press.

McKenna, M. (1998) The limits of evil and the role of moral address: a defense of Strawsonian compatibilism, *Journal of Ethics* 2(2): 123–42.

McKenna, M. (2006) Group responsibility and an agent meaning theory. In P. French and H. Wettstein (eds), *Midwest Studies in Philosophy, 30(1): Shared Intentions and Collective Responsibility*. Malden, MA: Wiley-Blackwell, pp. 16–34.

Meijers, A. (2003) Can collective intentionality be individualized? *American Journal of Economics and Sociology* 62(1): 167–83.

Menary, R. (2010) *The Extended Mind*. Cambridge, MA: MIT Press.

Miller, S. (1995) Intentions, ends and joint action, *Philosophical Papers* 24(1): 51–66.

Miller, S. (2001) *Social Action: A Teleological Account*. Cambridge: Cambridge University Press.

Miller, S. (2010) *The Moral Foundations of Social Institutions: A Philosophical Study*. Cambridge: Cambridge University Press.

Miller, S., and Makela, P. (2005) The collectivist approach to collective moral responsibility, *Metaphilosophy* 36(5): 634–51.

Millikan, R. G. (1995) Pushmi-pullyu representations, *Philosophical Perspectives* 9, AI: *Connectionism and Philosophical Psychology*: 185–200.

Mölder, B. (2010) *Mind Ascribed: An Elaboration and Defence of Interpretivism*. Philadelphia: John Benjamins.

Peacocke, C. (2005) Joint attention: its nature, reflexivity, and relation to common knowledge. In N. M. Eilan, C. Hoerl, T. McCormack, and J. Roessler (eds), *Joint Attention: Communication and Other Minds*. Oxford: Clarendon Press, pp. 298–324.

Pettit, P. (2003) Groups with minds of their own. In F. Schmitt (ed.), *Socializing Metaphysics*. Lanham, MD: Rowman & Littlefield, pp. 167–93.

Polger, T. (2009a) Evaluating the evidence for multiple realization, *Synthese* 167(3): 457–72.

Polger, T. (2009b) Identity theories, *Philosophy Compass* 4(5): 822–34.

Putnam, H. (1967) The nature of mental states. In W. H. Capitan and D. D. Merrill (eds), *Art, Mind, and Religion*. Pittsburgh: Pittsburgh University Press, pp. 37–48.

Quinton, A. (1976) Social objects, *Proceedings of the Aristotelian Society* 76: 1–27.

Ren, Y., and Argote, L. (2011) Transactive memory systems 1985–2010: an integrative framework of key dimensions, antecedents, and consequences, *Academy of Management Annals* 5(1): 189–229.

Roth, A. (2010) Shared agency, *Stanford Encyclopedia of Philosophy*, http://plato.stanford.edu/entries/shared-agency/.

Rovane, C. A. (1998) *The Bounds of Agency: An Essay in Revisionary Metaphysics*. Princeton, NJ: Princeton University Press.

Rovane, C. (2014) Group agency and individualism, *Erkenntnis*, http://link.springer.com/article/10.1007%2Fs10670-014-9634-9.

Rudoren, J., and Sanger, D. E. (2013) Israel says Syria has used chemical weapons, *Boston Globe*, April 23, www.bostonglobe.com/news/world/2013/04/23/israel-says-syria-has-used-chemical-weapons/DmOcMIbrZ3EDzUaJfwJ2rO/story.html.

Rupert, R. D. (2009) *Cognitive Systems and the Extended Mind*. Oxford: Oxford University Press.

Rupert, R. (2011) Empirical arguments for group minds: a critical appraisal, *Philosophy Compass* 6(9): 630–9.

Ryle, G. (1949) *The Concept of Mind*. London: Hutchinson.

Schmitt, F. (2014) Group belief and acceptance. In S. R. Chant, F. A. Hindriks and G. Preyer (eds), *From Individual to Collective Intentionality*. Oxford: Oxford University Press, pp. 61–96.

Schwiekard, D., and Schmid, H. B. (2013) Collective intentionality, *Stanford Encyclopedia of Philosophy*, http://plato.stanford.edu/entries/collective-intentionality/.

Searle, J. (1983) *Intentionality: An Essay in the Philosophy of Mind*. Cambridge: Cambridge University Press.

Searle, J. (1990) Group intentions and actions. In P. R. Cohen, J. L. Morgan, and M. E. Pollack (eds), *Intentions in Communication*. Cambridge, MA: MIT Press, pp. 401–15.

Searle, J. (2010) *Making the Social World: The Structure of Human Civilization*. New York: Oxford University Press.

Sheehy, P. (2006) Holding them responsible. In P. French and H. Wettstein (eds), *Midwest Studies in Philosophy, 30(1): Shared Intentions and Collective Responsibility*. Malden, MA: Wiley-Blackwell, pp. 74–93.

Silver, D. (2005) A Strawsonian defense of corporate moral responsibility, *American Philosophical Quarterly* 42(4): 279–95.

Smith, T. H. (2012). Group Agency: The Possibility, Design, and Status of Corporate Agents, by Christian List and Philip Pettit. *Mind* 121(482): 501–7.

Stern, Lawrence (1974) Freedom, blame, and the moral community, *Journal of Philosophy* 71(3): 72–84.

Stoutland, F. (1997) Why are philosophers of action so anti-social? In L. Alanen, S. Heinämaa, and T. Walgren (eds), *Commonality and Particularity in Ethics*. New York: St Martin's Press, pp. 45–75.

Stoutland, F. (2008) The ontology of social agency, *Analyse & Kritik* 30: 533–51.

Strawson, P. F. (1968) *Studies in the Philosophy of Thought and Action*. Oxford University Press.

Sullivan, S. (2013) Republican National Committee reaffirms opposition to gay marriage, *Washington Post*, April 12, www.washingtonpost.com/blogs/post-politics/wp/2013/04/12/republican-national-committee-reaffirms-opposition-to-gay-marriage/.

Surowiecki, J. (2004) *The Wisdom of Crowds*. New York: Doubleday.

Sutton, J., Harris, C. B., Keil, P. G., and Barnier, A. J. (2010) The psychology of memory, extended cognition, and socially distributed remembering, *Phenomenology and the Cognitive Sciences* 9(4): 521–60.

Szigeti, A. (2014) Are individualist accounts of collective responsibility morally deficient? In A. Konzelmann Ziv and H. B. Schmid (eds), *Institutions, Emotions, and Group Agents*. New York: Springer, pp. 329–42.

Theiner, G. (2011) *Res cogitans extensa: A Philosophical Defense of the Extended Mind Thesis*. Frankfurt am Main: Peter Lang.

Theiner, G. (2013) Transactive memory systems: a mechanistic analysis of emergent group memory, *Review of Philosophy and Psychology* 4(1): 65–89.

Theiner, G., and O'Connor, T. (2010) The emergence of group cognition. In A. Corradini and T. O'Connor (eds), *Emergence in Science and Philosophy*. New York: Routledge, pp. 78–117.

Theiner, G., Allen, C., and Goldstone, R. L. (2010) Recognizing group cognition, *Cognitive Systems Research* 11(4): 378–95.

Tollefsen, D. (2003) Participant reactive attitudes and collective responsibility, *Philosophical Explorations* 6(3): 218–34.

Tollefsen, D. (2005) Let's pretend! Joint action and young children, *Philosophy of the Social Sciences* 35(1): 75–97.

Townsend, L. (2013) Being and becoming in the theory of group agency, *Abstracta* 7(1): 39–53.

Tuomela, R. (1995) Group beliefs, *Synthese* 91(3): 285–318.

Tuomela, R. (2006) Joint intention: we mode and I mode. In P. French and H. Wettstein (eds), *Midwest Studies in Philosophy, 30(1): Shared Intentions and Collective Responsibility*. Malden, MA: Wiley-Blackwell, pp. 35–58.

Tuomela, R. (2013) *Social Ontology: Collective Intentionality and Group Agents*. New York: Oxford University Press.

Velasquez, M. G. (1983) Why corporations are not morally responsible for anything that they do, *Business and Professional Ethics Journal* 2(3): 1–18.

Velleman, J. D. (1997) How to share an intention, *Philosophy and Phenomenological Research* 57(1): 29–51.

Watson, G. (1987) Responsibility and the limits of evil. In Ferdinand Schoeman (ed.), *Responsibility, Character, and the Emotions*. Cambridge: Cambridge University Press, pp. 256–86.

Wegner, D. M. (1987) Transactive memory: a contemporary analysis of the group mind. In B. Mullen and G. R. Goethals (eds), *Theories of Group Behavior*. New York: Springer, pp. 185–208.

Wegner, D. M. (1995) A computer network model of human transactive memory, *Social Cognition* 13: 1–21.

Wegner, D. M., Erber, R., and Raymond, P. (1991) Transactive memory in close relationships, *Journal of Personality and Social Psychology* 61: 923–9.

Wegner, D. M., Giuliano, T., and Hertel, P. T. (1985) Cognitive interdependence in close relationships. In W. Ickes (ed.), *Compatible and Incompatible Relationships*. New York: Springer, pp. 253–76.

Wilson, R. (2001) Group-level cognition, *Philosophy of Science* 68(3): S262–S273.

Wilson, R. (2004) *Boundaries of the Mind: The Individual in the Fragile Sciences: Cognition*. Cambridge: Cambridge University Press.

Wilson, R. (2005) Collective memory, group minds, and the extended mind thesis. *Cognitive Processing* 6(4): 227–36.

Wray, K. B. (2001) Collective belief and acceptance, *Synthese* 129(3): 319–33.

Zawidzki, T. (forthcoming) Dennett's strategy for naturalizing intentionality: an innovative play at 2nd base.

Index